Indigenized / Tribalized

Poems

By

Nishi Chawla

Published by Human Error Publishing
www.humanerrorpublishing.com
paul@humanerrorpublishing.com

Copyright © 2025
by
Human Error Publishing
&
Nishi Chawla

ISBN: 978-1-948521-25-3

Front Cover Photo Nishi Chawla
Design
Nishi Chawla & Human Error Publishing

Some of Nishi Chawla's poems here
have been previously published.

Human Error Publishing asks that no part of this publication be reproduced or transmitted in any form or by any means electronic or mechanical, including photocopy, recording or information storage or retrieval system without permission in writing from Nishi Chawla and Human Error Publishing. We ask that you support independent publishers and the writers.

"I am part of the land, and the land is part of me." - Inuit Saying

"The land is the mother, and we are of the earth. We do not own the land; the land owns us." - Aboriginal Australian Proverb

"They tried to bury us. They didn't know we were seeds." - Mexican Proverb

"The forest is our mother, the river our bloodline, and the sky our witness. To take from the land is to take from ourselves." - Adivasi Proverb

Table of Contents

First Rights   10
The Cartographers of Loss   12
Indigenous Poem   14
The Dismantling   16
Erosion   18
Unfenced Horizons   19

Americas: Survival of the Land
Last Song of the Earth   23
The Sioux Walk -   25
Dispersed into Sky   27
The Seminole's Echo   29
Tuskaloosa's Forgotten Breath   31
Diné Bloodlines Under the Desert Sky   33
Acoma: Sky Holds Their Breath   35
Zuni: The River Knows Their Name   37
Taos: Where the Mountain Breathes   39
Principal People   41
Silent Exodus of Laguna   42
Beneath the Red Earth   43
In the cradle of the Rio Grande   45
The Mescalero   46
A Fluid Path   47
Sequoyah's Song   49
Keresan   51
Keresan: The River That Speaks   52
Flames of the Desert   54
Within the Concrete Forest   56
Sacred Ice: Inuit Whispers in Alaska   60

Voices of the North: The Arctic and Subarctic: Between Ice and Fire
Voices of the Land: The First Nations of Canada   65
Blood of Two Rivers   70
The Arctic Breath of the Inuit   73
The Ones Who Walk with Reindeer   77

The Breath of Sápmi	80
The People Who Speak the Land	84
Chukchi: Bone, Ice, and Breath	86
The Sea's Quiet Witness	88

Through the Canopy: Indigenous Voices of South and Central America

The Ancient Souls of the Arawak	93
Yanomami	96
Mapuche: We Who Do Not Bow	97
Quechua: The Stone and the Sky	100
The Glyphs Remember	102

Nomads, Shamans, and First Peoples: Asia's Indigenous Heritage

Adivasis	107
Gond Songs Shaping the Earth	109
The Santhals Who Walked First	111
The Bhils Move Like Rivers	114
Buffalo Songs in the Nilgiris	116
Earth Remembers Oraon Footsteps	118
Driftwood and Ancestors	120
Breath of the Heights	121
No Songs Left for the Tharus	122
Hmong, We Weave	125
Sky-Bound Riders	128
The Ones Who Hold the Sky	129

Africa: Rhythms of the Earth

The Red Thread of the Maasai	131
Beating Heart of the Zulu	132
Ancestral Drums of Yoruba	134
Voices of the Kalahari	136
The Unwritten Map of the Amazigh	138
Igbo: The Ones Who Refuse to Vanish	139
Stone and Sound: The Shona	141
Himba Do Not Vanish	143
The Sabar Beats for the Wolof	145

Ochre Hands, Timeless Lands:
Aboriginal Echoes from Australia
Whakapapa: The Blood of the Māori   149
Tattooed in the Bones of Samoa   151
The Palawa Are Still Here   153
The Noongar Dreaming: Boodja's Breath   154
Fiji's Silent Song   155
Tonga: The Weight of Names   157

Resistance and Survival:
The Struggle for Rights

The Ones Who Walk Before the Road   161
Borrowed From Tomorrow   163
Voices Beneath the Soil   164
The Forest Breathes Them   165
Resistance and Survival   166
Infinite Hearth ß   168

First Rights

The land does not speak in words
But in the language of ash and sap,
Its vowels the curve of an elk's antler,
Its consonants the hum of stones
Worn smooth by countless knees.

A birch tree remembers
Hands tracing its bark
A lover memorizing skin
Not to own,
But to learn what it means to belong.

Rivers do not flow;
They bleed,
Their paths dark sutures
Binding the earth's tender wounds,
Each ripple a gasp,
Each current a whisper,
We were here before thirst was named.

Mountains do not rise;
They coil inward,
Their spines arching in silent defiance,
Hoarding the sky for those
Who knew its weight in stars
Before it was traded for wires.

What is a boundary
To the wind that knows
The salt of every ocean,
The musk of every pine?
It slips through fence posts,
Gathers the embers of crushed sage,
And carries it like a hymn.

First rights are not seen;
They are the shadow
Cast by a flame long extinguished,
The smell of cedar smoke
Lingering in a hollowed-out cave

Where echoes refuse to fade.

The Cartographers of Loss

They mapped the land with footsteps,
names unbroken like river veins,
whispering syllables of rain and bone,
until the ink of conquest rewrote the sky.

First, they came with questions
their voices clothed in barter,
measuring the land in lengths of greed,
asking where the forests ended,
where the minerals bled from stone.
Then, they came with answers
fences driven into the ribs of earth,
the air weighted with deeds and borders,
as if paper could hold back the wind.

The cedar split, the buffalo fell,
the salt of the sea was christened with new names.
In the red dust of Australia, a mother
clutched the absence of her child
taken, renamed, reshaped in the mouth of empire.
In the Amazon, an elder walked into a jungle
he no longer knew, where the trees
wore numbers instead of spirits.
On the tundra, the caribou changed their path,
searching for a world before fences.

In the forests of Jharkhand,
the Santhal woman ran her fingers
along the earth's pulse,
but where the *sal* trees once stood,
now only chimneys coughed up smoke.
In Bastar, the Gond hunter traced
his grandfather's bow,
but the iron mines had swallowed
the paths of his ancestors.
The Narmada carried their songs once,
until the dam silenced its voice,
leaving villages drowned in mouth of progress.

Across the ocean, the Cherokee walked
a trail of tears across their own land,
their footprints vanishing under treaties

that tasted of dust and betrayal.
The Lakota prayed at Wounded Knee,
where the wind still howled with
the voices of the fallen.
The Diné wove their stories into rugs,
patterns of resistance hidden
in the warp and weft of exile.

And what of the songs?
They curled at the edges like burning hide,
pounded into silence beneath schoolyard desks,
buried under church steeples
that rang with another god's voice.
Children were taught to say their own names
as if apologizing.

Everywhere, the rivers were forced backward,
the earth stitched with pipelines and rails,
the sky cleaved by turbines
that did not know the language of wings.
Yet the elders still touch the ground,
listening for the heartbeat beneath.
They hold stories in their hands,
cupped like water,
offering the past to mouths too young
to remember their own echoes.

To be displaced is to be unthreaded,
yet the hands that wove the first baskets
still carry memory in their palms.
The cedar will regrow.
The buffalo will return.
The river, unchained, will remember its name.

They cannot steal the footsteps.
They cannot silence the earth.
Even the wind, unsettled,
still speaks in the old tongue.

Indigenous Poem

They walk where the earth speaks
in a language older than wind,
where rivers braid their voices
with the sorrow of forests,
where mountains wear shadows
like ancestral cloaks.
They walk in the margins
a world that has forgotten how to listen.

Once, their feet pressed the soil
with a knowing deeper than maps,
charting paths by constellations,
bird calls, rustling leaves.
Then the cities rose
metal spines piercing land's tender flesh,
ambition severing root from earth.

Now, they dwell at the edges,
behind fences of law and disdain.
Their histories spill into forgotten dialects,
stories the modern tongue cannot shape.
They carry their homes in their bones,
homes that exist in the smoke rings of memory.

The world calls them relics
treasures locked behind glass,
lessons buried in books
written by hands
that have never held displacement.

Yet they remain
rivers that refuse to dry,
seeds cast on soil
that denies them water.
They sing against silence,
dance in defiance of forgetting,
their grief repackaged, art sold as trinkets,
their suffering archived
as if colonization ended
with the last treaty signed.

And yet, they endure.
Carving existence from stone,
weaving baskets from dreams
that refuse to fray.
They summon the names of spirits
modern tongues have lost.
They teach their children
to listen to the earth
even as bulldozers
muffle its voice.

Their struggles are not metaphors.
They are the ache in the land's backbone,
the howl of wolves displaced by concrete,
the hunger of a people
fighting erasure with fire in their eyes.

They walk where the earth still whispers,
even as the wind carries the noise
of a world that will not see them.
They walk where roots hold the past,
where every step
is both a prayer for what remains
and a cry for what has been lost.

The Dismantling

A language unspoken does not die
It frays
in the mouth of a child

who answers in the language of the school,
in the silence of a grandmother

who understands but no longer teaches.

A name, sanded down for convenience,
no longer fits the curve of land it once belonged.
It is filed away,
archived in census records,
written but not spoken.

Hands that once carved stories into stone
now press buttons,
fill forms,
sign away parcels of land for

something called opportunity.

A river bends toward what is left of itself,
carrying a name that no longer belongs to it.
Tourists kneel at its edge,
take pictures of the reflection
without asking what was lost beneath the surface.

They build museums for what still breathes,
turn history into artifacts,
safety glass between the past and the present.

Somewhere, a fire burns low,
in a village that no longer knows its borders.
The smoke, heavy with unfamiliar oils,
blends with the blue-less sky
a symbol no one remembers how to read.

Outside, the wind calls in the old way.
No one answers.

Erosion

They call it progress,
a road carved through the spine of a mountain,
a school where the children no longer speak
in the rhythm of their ancestors.

The old songs are whispered now,
pressed between the pages of history books
that no one reads aloud.

A grandmother folds the last of dyed threads,
her loom silenced,
its echoes replaced by factory hum.

A boy, once named for the river,
responds to something easier to pronounce,
something that fits neatly
on a form stamped with approval.

In the city, someone wears a feather in their hair,
calls it fashion,
forgets the hands that once carried the weight
of its meaning.

A shadow moves over forgotten soil,
fingers brushing what was once held sacred.
No eyes remain to witness its path.

Yet something stirs in the deep,
hidden from who walk the surface,
a tremor that speaks in a tongue
the earth has not forgotten.

And the land, stripped of its names,
waits in quiet rebellion,
knowing that roots remember
what tongues forget.

Unfenced Horizons

The first vibration,
hum before language,
echo of earth dreaming itself into form,
memory the body carries
being cradled in soil,
recognition between breath and wind,
silent pact between heartbeat and horizon.

Ground that thinks beneath us,
consciousness holds mountains and rivers
extensions of its own rhythm
not built,
but unveiled,
a presence older than time,
wider than any boundary,
deeper than exile.

Not possession,
but participation.
A living covenant,
treaty between hunger and harvest,
between grief and the patience of stone,
between breath and the infinite patience of sky.
A fire that does not die,
embers carried across deserts, seas, and exile,
seeking soil willing to receive them.

Colonial maps tried to draw borders around it,
to rename, divide, quantify;
home, for Indigenous peoples, resists contraction,
larger than the surveyor's hand,
older than the census taker's ink,
more fluid than the conqueror's fence.

To speak of home
is to speak of the mountain that cannot be sold,
the river that carries memory in its flow,
the animal whose migration writes scripture,
the tree that has heard more prayers
than any temple built of stone.

Home is continuity:
ancestor, present, and unborn child
braided together by ritual and land.
It is where the Diné mountains still rise,
where the Gond murals still speak,
where the Lakota sky still arches,
where the Santhal drums still summon,
where the Cherokee syllables still ignite flame.

Not behind us,
not ahead
home is the eternal present,
stretching across continents,
refusing erasure,
teaching us,
if we listen,
that belonging is never ownership,
but remembrance.

Americas: Survival of the Land

Last Song of the Earth

From stone-skinned mountains of the North
Where the winds carry names of ancestors,
Earth hums beneath feet of those who remember.
Their hands are carved by the soil,
Fingers stained with ink of sacred rivers.
These hands held the first fire,
The smoke still rises in veins of land,
Whispering the songs that have no end.

In the desert's heart, where sun sculpts silence,
The cactus carries stories in its spines,
Its roots sunk deep into forgotten realms.
Sand remembers dance of rain that never came,
And the sky still holds weight of prayers,
Woven into the constellations of birthright.
Echoes ripple across dry valleys,
Stirring bones of old nations never lost.

In ancient places where trees bend with age
Rivers run with the blood of the earth,
Forests speaks in tongues of bark and vine,
A language older than the first storm.
Roots entwine like forgotten hands,
Hold the memory of battles fought in shadows,
harvests reaped without greed,
sacred spaces where fireflies are stars' children.

Between the snow and the desert's heat,
From hills where the eagle's shadow slices the sky,
rivers that snake across the land's spine,
tribes breathe the same breath as the wind,
and the wind has no home.
Voice of those who walk without fear of forgetting.

Across mountains, valleys, and plains,
Drums beat with rhythm of earth's heartbeat,

But earth is no longer silent.
It is awake, it remembers.
And the people
are the pulse within its blood.

They speak in colors painted on rock faces,
In songs that travel with the birds' flight,
Steps that leave no trace but imprint of the soul,
Carving paths into the ground
With the weight of their ancestors' footsteps.

These tribes,
Woven into the fabric of time,
Are not echoes. They are the stamp
Of a continent that refuses to forget,
Even as the world turns
And the land stretches,
Endlessly,
Toward the horizon
Where the first stars bled into earth's skin.

The Sioux Walk

They move in the marrow of the land,
names shaped by the wind that bends grass.
Dakota, where rivers carve old songs into stone,
Nakota, where the sky opens wider than eye,
Lakota, where the plains stretch, unbroken,
to the edge of knowing.
Not a map's border, not a treaty's ink
but a breath, a lineage of footsteps
that do not vanish when the buffalo fall.

Beneath the vast, whispering sky
the earth calls, not with words,
but with the tremors of stone
and the voice of unseen rivers
that have always known their names.

The wind wraps around fingers of ancestors,
invisible thread stretching across centuries,
binding breath to mountain,
footprint to valley,
hands to the dust that once fed the roots
of trees now only dreams
of ones who had kissed their bark.

Their homes rose and fell with the land,
tipis fold like hands in prayer, opening to sky and storm.
No walls to contain the wind,
no doors to keep the earth out. Only
poles and hide, light enough to follow buffalo's path.
At dawn, the Sun Dance stretched flesh toward sky,
pain threading the body to the world beyond sight.
Alone on a ridge, a vision seeker waited,
emptied of hunger, filled with breath of land,
listening for whisper that carves his path into time.

Earth was not a thing to be owned,
but a rhythm to follow.

They moved with the thunder of hooves,
the dark currents of buffalo herds,
carry homes like the wind carries a promise.
Firelight carved their voices into the night,
stories passing from tongue to tongue,
not written, but rooted, not owned, but lived.
In the hush before dawn,
a dancer lifted his face to the sun,
a seeker traced the edges of a vision,
both listen for breath of land speaking back.

Sioux walk on a path older than memory,
woven into the heartbeat of the earth,
rhythm too ancient to be spoken,
only felt,
like the quiet thunder of buffalo hooves
that once darkened the horizon
with a promise of survival,
now scattered as whispers in the wind.

Their bones sing to the stones,
Their songs ripple through the rivers,
as if the water carries within it
the ghosts of ancestors
whose faces no longer need be remembered
because they are already here,
woven into the skin of the earth,
woven into the heart of the Sioux.

In the silence of the plains,
the land hums the story of a people
who are not separate from it,
but the very soil itself,
the sky and the flame
that burns when the sun sets.
They are the breath of the wind,
the crackling of fire,
the shadow of the great eagle.

Dispersed into Sky

The mountains are not innocent.
They watched everything,
crags carved by weight of a people's footsteps,
valleys filled with the silence left behind.
Granite does not cry,
but it splits,
jagged edges speak the language of fracture.

Buffalo trails once braided the plains,
wide enough to carry histories -
now, only the thin etching of fences remains,
a barbed whisper
slicing the wind into pieces.

Smoke from the council fires
once twisted itself into shape of meaning,
a silent treaty with the sky.
Now the sky has forgotten its promises,
trading clouds for contrails,
stars for artificial light.

Chilkat blankets draped shoulders
like rivers finding their course,
now lie folded in museums,
flattened artifacts
as if meaning could be confined to glass cases.

The rivers fled too
not south, but deeper into themselves,
hiding their voices beneath frozen rapids,
their echoes locked in an ice
that does not thaw in memory.

The grasslands stretched forever,
unbroken and whole,
until the iron horse came,
its belly full of steam and greed,
its breath scattering elk and song alike.

What happened to the tribes of Colorado?
Ask the red dirt,
still warm from the friction of treaties burned
and homes uprooted.

Ask the wind,
which carries their prayers westward,
where the sun hides its face
behind the peaks
that knew them first.

They carved names into stone,
not their own,
etching roads over bones
that still shift beneath pavement.
What was solid, they made hollow,
what was sacred, they sold.

Listen at dusk, the ground
hums when it thinks no one is watching,
the voices that once filled the canyons
rise in the breath of sage.
Not lost.
Only waiting.

The Seminole's Echo

The swamp remembers,
not the way rivers forget in their rush to the sea,
but in the slow, brackish churn of mangroves
clutching at water like a mother who won't let go.

A horizon of sawgrass sings low,
its voice a rippling ache.
the tremor of feet that ran
when treaties became kindling,
their promises curling into ash.

Hunger does not walk here;
it crawls, on the bellies of gators,
slick and patient,
beneath the broken moonlight
that once guided them through Everglades' maze.

The land swallowed them whole,
not as conquest,
but as shelter,
its belly a fortress of roots and shadow.

They became whispers in palmettos,
names carved into the breath of hurricanes,
faces painted in the eyes of panthers
that roam as if carrying their ghosts.

Even the cypress stands taller for them,
arms stretched upward
not to beg,
but to demand memory.

Where are they now?
A question the sand cannot answer,
its grains holding too many fragments,
each too sharp to grasp.

In the marsh,
an egret takes flight,
its wings dragging the weight of stories
it will never be able to tell.

The fire does not die.

It smolders in the stomp dance,
feet drumming messages into earth,
voices rising like the slow-build of thunder,
a circle unbroken, even when the world
tried to break them.

Hands carve the river's wisdom into palmetto,
weaving stories tight as a grandmother's grip,
patterns winding through time,
stitching memory into black-dyed fabric,
each thread a silent refusal to vanish.

The wind carries their language,
not lost, but waiting in the throat of the heron,
in the hush of dugout canoes
skimming the mirrored water,
in the stomp of moccasins
against a land that still knows their name.

The words do not fade.
They press into cypress bark,
spill from the mouths of water,
held in the hush between frog calls and wind.
Not just sound, but shape
the way lips form survival,
the way elders carve meaning into breath,
so even silence speaks their name.

Tuskaloosa's Forgotten Breath

The Tuskagee do not vanish
they are folded
pressed like leaves into spine of books
no one remembers how to open.

History bleeds in whispers.
Their footprints were not erased,
but layered over
mud thick with labor of borrowed hands,
feet that built roads for other nations' dreams.

The soil hums low,
an ache born from centuries of friction,
where stories were plowed under
to plant cotton,
to grow silence.

Who hears the drumbeat
of broken treaties?
A sound that cannot ripple in still air,
but finds its home in the cracked throats
of rivers searching for their mouths.

Time turns black,
like the char of a cooking fire long abandoned,
embers dusted over by progress,
by forgetting,
by maps drawn with shaky, foreign hands.

Did you know the wind can hold grief?
It wraps around the oak trees
their ancestors leaned against,
listening for voices that will never come back.

They are not ghosts.
They are the smell of earth after rain,
the way moss grows soft against stone,
the thin crack in a cedar canoe
floating further,
further.

When you touch the ground in Alabama,
your hands touch theirs,

buried not in death
but in a kind of waiting
only the land understands.

The river still knows their songs,
not the ones written down,
but those hummed between cedar ribs,
paddles dipping, lifting,
like hands blessing the water.

Corn remembers their touch,
how it was sung into harvest,
braided into prayers,
set by the fire to listen
as elders shaped history with their tongues.

Their hands carved stories in clay,
not to be displayed behind glass,
but to be used
bowls deep enough to hold hunger,
cups wide enough for the sky.

Diné Bloodlines Under Desert Sky

The Navajo Nation stretches,
not like a map,
but like the skin of the earth pulled taut,
wrinkled in sandstone, veined with
arroyos that quicken only when it rains.

Red earth remembers imprint of moccasins,
paths etched by ancestors whose shadows
still cling to the cliffs,
their whispers caught in the spiral of the wind.

Hogan walls breathe,
their wood and mud
holding the scent of cedar smoke
and the weight of stories -
stars born in mouths of grandmothers.

Canyons do not echo like they should;
they hoard voices,
folding them into their folds,
a quiet archive
of chants, war cries, and laughter.

Sheep graze against backdrop of monuments
carved by gods whose names are now prayers,
while their wool holds the colors of the land -
ochre, charcoal, bone -
woven into patterns that map survival.

The sky stretches wide,
too wide for memory to escape,
and yet, there are silences
spaces where uranium mines poisoned ground,
where treaties turned to dust
before they reached the elders' hands.

But the Diné endure:
like the juniper rooted in rock,
drinking from invisible springs.
Even the sun pauses,
rising gently over Shiprock,
as if paying respect
to those who name it Tse Bit'a'í

the winged one that guards their horizon.

They carry their world in a basket:
not woven from willow,
but from their language,
their ceremonies,
their prayers, each strand
hold balance, four sacred mountains.

Under the Milky Way,
they walk the path of the Holy People,
their footsteps soft,
their songs louder than history.

Acoma: Sky Holds Their Breath

The Acoma Pueblo rises,
not built, but grown,
a mesa-born city
where earth and sky shake hands.
Adobe wall carries colors of morning,
sunlight baked into its skin,
a hymn of ochre and quiet endurance.

There are no stairs to the sky city,
only the memory of hands
that carved trails into stone,
paths that knew the weight of water jars
and prayers ascending in silence.

Rain is not just rain here.
It is the blood of clouds,
A blessing drawn thin in the desert air,
Each drop a promise the earth swallows whole.
When it falls,
It carries the scent of history,
A musky echo of seeds sown, unsown.

Pottery holds the world's curvature,
its surface painted in patterns
that mimic the migration of winds,
the flight of swallows,
the spiral of the universe
spun on a wheel of human hands.

The land whispers secrets:
that sandstone was once ocean,
that the cliffs remember
the voices of women grinding corn,
turning stone to powder,
grains to gold.

But the Acoma know
the weight of waiting.
For centuries,
they stood at the edge of cliffs,
watching invaders crawl across the plains,
their armor glinting like broken promises.
The earth trembled then,

not with fear,
but with rage,
its stones sharp with resistance.

And still they remain
the people who call themselves
Haak'u,
a place prepared.
They live with the patience of rock,
weathering winds that try to scatter,
enduring under the weight of sky.

The stars bow low here,
their light brushing the roofs
where elders sit,
their words braided into the night's fabric.
Every breath the Acoma take
is tethered to the horizon,
an inhale of spirit, breath of stone,
an exhale of belonging.

This is not a city.
This is the earth dreaming of itself,
a reflection of the sacred balance
between stone, sky, and the hands
that refuse to let either fall.

Zuni: River Knows Their Name

Zuni move like water
river winding through time,
carving the land with stories
too fluid to be held by maps.
Their home is not a place;
it is a current,
a breath of earth and spirit
braided into turquoise veins.

Mountains rise around them,
not as walls,
but as elders,
their spines cracked with wisdom,
their shadows long enough
to shelter the past.
Every peak carries the scent of corn pollen,
an offering to the sky
that answers in bursts of rain.

Kachinas do not sleep;
they wait in the wings of birds,
in the shadows of stones,
their dance etched
into the rhythm of the land.
The people follow their steps
not with their feet,
but with their hearts,
echoing the beat of the drum.

Salt trails stretch into the desert,
a pilgrimage of reverence,
where the feet of ancestors
still press lightly into the earth,
each step a quiet vow.
Here, the air tastes of ceremony
ashes, rain, the sharp edge of enduring.

Their hands remember clay's language,
shaping earth into vessels
that carry not water,
but worlds.
Each pot a constellation of meaning,

its designs whispers the flight of spirits,
twist of rivers,
the way the sun breaks through storm clouds.

Zuni know
that the wind is a storyteller.
It carries voices across the mesas,
tangles them in the sagebrush,
and lays them at the feet of those who listen.
Even the rocks speak
if you sit long enough,
their silence a translation
of cycles too vast to measure.

This is not a story of survival.
This is a story of roots,
of finding water in the deepest cracks,
of knowing that the desert is alive
and listening.

Zuni endure,
not as remnants,
but as rivers,
as seeds,
as fire carried from hearth to hearth.
Their name is not a word;
it is the hum of life itself,
resonating in the spaces
between sky and stone.

Taos: Where the Mountain Breathes

The mountain does not stand still.
It inhales,
pulling clouds into its ribs,
its breath stitching snow
to the shoulders of the earth.
The Taos live in its exhale,
where the air tastes of pine sap
and the quiet sound of snowmelt.

Adobe walls lean into the land,
not separate from it
but growing out of the earth's skin,
sun-warmed and river-smoothed.
Each crack is a vein,
each shadow a memory.
They do not call it architecture;
they call it home.

Red Willow Creek hums softly,
thread unraveling from heart of the world,
its waters folding over stones
the way hands fold over prayers.
It carries the weight of voices,
whispered chants,
laughter braided into the current.

Drums beat like thunder caught in a circle,
their rhythm too vast for the ears alone.
It sinks into the soles of feet,
into the marrow of bones,
a pulse that remembers
the first morning light
spilling over the Sangre de Cristo peaks.

The kiva descends into the earth,
a womb where fire speaks.
Its smoke curls upward,
a silent messenger
spiraling toward the sun,
meaning caught in the wings of hawks.

Here, the sky wears turquoise and amber,
a shifting, fluid canvas, painterly,
that unravels at dusk,
only to be rewoven by dawn.
The people watch it stretch
across the peaks,
knowing that each shade of light
holds a lesson
too large for language.

They speak to the deer,
not with words,
but with soft gesture of offering,
a bow to the balance
that ties the hunter to the hunted,
the living to the land.

This is not survival.
This is symbiosis.
Roots intertwining with stories,
hands shaping clay
as the clay shapes them,
the mountain breathing life
into the people who call it sacred.

At night,
stars crowd the sky,
leaning close
as if to hear the quiet songs
of those who know
that the world is alive
and that every stone,
every tree,
every shadow,
remembers.

Principal People

They are the breath of mountain rivers,
folding through mossy arms of trees,
whisper what remains of a language once flowing
like the red clay beneath the wild water.
Their footsteps linger in the air,
ancient dust rising from the earth
as the wind pulls through the hollows,
humming stories only the rocks can understand.

The Cherokee hold time not as a line,
but as a circle,
days and nights lean against each other,
their edges softened by the moon's hand.
Between the cedar's smell and the fire's crackle,
each heartbeat echoing across valleys
where the spirit of the land is still too sacred
to be spoken by any tongue but the river's.

In their eyes are the smoke of old fires,
their silence holds the weight of forests unseen,
where every tree, every stone,
has worn the memory of a thousand ancestors,
not forgotten,
but waiting,
waiting like a seed in the soil
for the right moment to break through again.

They are the sky above,
unbroken by time's sharp edges,
and they are the earth below,
gathering roots in the dark places
where only those who truly listen
can hear the stories of the Cherokee,
not as myths,
but as breath,
as truth
beneath the skin of the world.

Silent Exodus of Laguna

Earth trembles, weight of forgotten footsteps,
Sun's gaze turns away, the land's ancient embrace.
Sky, once a canvas of ancestral songs,
Now bears the scars of imposed silence.
Wind carries the smell of distant lands,
Soil remains parched, cracked
like the memories of a people uprooted.
River's song is muted,
Its waters diverted,
Its path altered by hands that do not know its name.
Mountains stand as silent witnesses,
Peaks obscured by the dust of displacement.
Stars, once familiar guides,
Now flicker uncertainly in a foreign sky.
The hearths are cold,
Fires of tradition extinguished,
People scatter like seeds in a storm,
Seeking soil that will not yield.
Horizon stretches endlessly,
Line that promises return but offers none.
Land calls out,
Its voice is lost in the confusion of change.
The people endure,
Roots entwined in the bones of the earth,
Their spirit unbroken, waiting for the day
when the land will remember them.

Beneath the Red Earth

In the dark gut of the arid mesas,
The sun's relentless gaze burns the skin of the earth,
The Hopis wait, yawn, resist, stand red rock infused,
Their eyes reflect the weight of tortured centuries.
Their hands, carved, weathered, calloused,
Hold the stories of a people, roots run deep in the red soil.

In the dry embrace of the mesas' arms,
Where clouds are sparse, and rain a charm,
The Hopis turn to ancient ways,
To coax the earth in its sunlit haze.

With sticks they carve the hardened crust,
Into the soil where they place their trust.
Corn, beans, and squash in deep-set beds,
Drink dew and dreams where the water treads.

They sing to the seeds, a sacred refrain,
A whisper of hope to summon the rain.
Each furrow a prayer, each sprout a vow,
The Hopis thrive where others ask how.

Even in drought, their faith persists,
The spirit of dry farming resists.
A wisdom born from land and sky,
In the arid heart, the Hopis defy.

Their hands remember, their hearts endure,
For the land and its voice are ancient, pure.
And though conquest loomed and rivers wept,
The Hopis' bond with the soil is kept.

The mesas stand, scarred weight of forgotten prayers,
Their surfaces etched, silent screams of ancestors.
Once, the land was a living canvas,
Painted with colors of corn and the songs of the wind.

Now, it is a hollow shell,
Its bones picked clean by the vultures of conquest.
The kivas lie in ruins,
Their sacred walls crumbled, dreams of a people displaced.

The hearths are cold,
Flames of tradition extinguished by icy breath of foreign hands.
The cornfields barren, their
Roots severed by the plow of colonization.

The rivers run dry,
Their waters diverted to quench the thirst of invaders.
The sky is a canvas of ash,
Its stars obscured, smoke of burning villages.

The songs are silenced,
Melodies lost in the cacophony of oppression.
The Hopi people live on,
their spirits unbroken,
Their hearts beat in rhythm with the earth,
Wait for the day when the land will remember them.

In the cradle of the Rio Grande

In the cradle of the Rio Grande,
the Santa Ana Pueblo stands,
its adobe walls whispering tales of recusance.
The earth beneath their feet, red and ochre,
woven with the threads, their ancestors' hands.
Their language, Keresan, flows like the river,
a song of the land,
a melody of the spirit.

To the north, rises the Santa Clara Pueblo,
Its cliffs etched with stories of time.
The land, a mosaic of canyons and mesas,
Each stone a chapter,
Each shadow a verse.
Their Tewa tongue dances in the wind,
Rain tracing the grooves of ancient stone,
An unquiet hymn.

Pueblos unbent, vessels of tradition,
Pottery adorned, symbols of cosmos,
Dancing prayers to wild elements.
Their paths diverging, language they speak,
The songs they sing, sanctify.
The stories they tell, suggest.
One speaks syllables, the river's journey,
The other of the low mountain's ascent.

In the heart of the earth,
their roots intertwine,
a silent testament to their shared heritage.
Though their voices are distinct,
their spirits are one,
echoing in the canyons,
whispering in the winds,
dancing in the flames.

The Mescalero

In the cradle of Sierra Blanca's embrace,
the Mescalero tread softly,
their footsteps a whisper on the wind.
From the heart of the agave,
they draw sustenance
the mescal plant, their namesake,
its fibers woven into the fabric of their lives.

Once, they roamed the vast expanse,
hunters and gatherers,
masters of the chase,
their horses swift as the desert breeze.
In the dance of the *Gaan*,
they seek the Mountain Spirits,
a prayer for health, for harmony,
their movements, silent song to the earth.

Now, beneath the sacred peaks,
the Inn of the Mountain Gods stands,
an odd monument, a paradox
where the past and present converge.
The Mescalero endure,
their spirit unbroken,
their story etched in the land,
a legacy of strength, of survival,
echoing through the canyons,
whispering on the wind.

Arid expanse of southeastern New Mexico,
The land stretches wide,
Canvas of sagebrush and mesquite,
The sun paints earth, hues of gold and crimson.
The wind carries tales of ancient times,
Whistling through the canyons,
Dancing with the dust,
The Mescalero Apache are born again, in rebirth.

A Fluid Path

Beneath the vast, unbroken sky,
where winds hum songs of ages past,
the Jicarilla Apache roam,
footprints fleeting in the sands of time.

From the plains, where grasses whisper,
to the forests, where shadows breathe,
they wander, as their ancestors did,
seeking the pulse of the earth beneath.

With bow and arrow, with hand and heart,
they trace the rhythms of the wild,
hunting the stag, gathering the berry,
raiding to reclaim what was once denied.

The mountains, jagged and cold,
speak of struggle, of sacred lore,
yet in each stone and each stream,
they find the wisdom of ancestors' dreams.

No chain could bind their spirit free,
no boundary could hold their claim,
for they are the wind and the river,
flowing where the seasons change.

Rain and drought, peace and war,
Moving with the rhythms of the land,
Fluid as the clouds that drift and dissolve,
Rooted in the soil of their ancestors' hands.

And though their paths may shift and scatter,
their hearts remain ever strong,
for the Jicarilla Apache are the land,
and the land, they've always belonged.

Their language holds the shape of rivers,
words bending, reshaping, never still,

syllables tracing the flight of hawks,
the curve of an antler, the hush of dawn.

In the glow of the morning fire,
hands paint stories on rawhide drums,
voices rise with cedar smoke,
calling ancestors back through time.

Their words, born of the Southern winds,
dance like firelight on canyon walls,
each syllable a thread of memory,
woven into stories that refuse to fall.
Through classrooms, songs, whispered prayers,
they teach the young to speak the old,
reviving a tongue that holds the soul,
a river of wisdom, timeless and bold.

In the circle of the sacred flame,
their spirits rise, their hearts entwine,
through healing chants, dances aflame,
they honor earth, the divine design.
The stars bear witness, the drums resound,
each step, a bond with the sacred ground.
Surviving as the mountains they roam,
their ceremonies make the spirit home.

Sequoyah's Song

Before rivers learned to speak in currents,
before the wind rehearsed its endless hymns,
Sequoyah gave his people a new breath -
marks pressed into bark,
curves and strokes alive with thought.
Each symbol a thread,
tying memory to voice,
voice to the bone of the earth.

From silence, a language unfurled -
a fire of glyphs rising like wings,
a way for stories to outlive the tongue.
The Phoenix of print smoldered,
but wisdom walked from ash to page,
each sign a doorway
to knowledge that would not die.

Seven clans grew as branches of one tree -
Wolf, Deer, Bird,
Wild Potato holding the soil,
Paint and Blue staining the sky,
Long Hair trailing rivers of kinship.
Together they shaped a circle
where belonging carried weight and breath.

In the hills, the ground drums softly,
its pulse felt beneath bare soles.
Soil is no dust but the face of ancestors,
creased with the long patience of time.
Trees stand like tall prayers,
leaves whispering care into the wind.
Roots tunnel toward the unseen,
seeking the marrow of origins.

Mountains lean against the sky,
not stone but the shoulders of kin.

Morning mist rises from their lungs,
a shawl of breath
wrapped around eagle and horizon alike.
Streams vein the earth with silver,
their waters gathered in the hand of a mother.
Every ripple remembers the covenant -
to nourish, to endure, to honor.

The wind does not pass without meaning.
It bends the grasses into bowing forms,
its movement a liturgy of respect.
To walk here is to enter a hymn,
the ground a living scripture,
shadow and limb interwoven with spirit.

Then came the breaking -
a trail where rivers choked on grief,
where silence pressed its weight
into every emptied step.
Exile carved itself into Cherokee body,
yet even along that long dying,
the song carried.

Stones remember,
each seed insists on return.
The land remains a temple,
keeper of promises,
the creed of a people who endure.

Keresan

It is not a language, rather a river,
Carving red canyons into the soul of the earth,
Its syllables bending like water
Around the stones of time.

Sound of smoke rising from adobe hearths,
Hum of cornfields kissed by desert wind,
Murmur of footsteps tracing
Ceremonial circle of ancestors.

Keresan, a fingerprint pressed into clay,
Every word a spiral etched by ancient hands,
Marking the unheard stories of stars,
Seasons, and unseen migrations.

It carries the weight of mesas and sky,
Its structure as jagged and alive
As the cliffs of Acoma,
Where prayers are built into walls
And vowels hold the scent of juniper.

The language does not speak.
It grows,
Rooted in sand and memory,
Its branches cast shades
Over generations
Who walk between sun and shadow.

To lose it
Would be to unravel the spirit,
To silence the thunder of distant drums,
To still the breath of a people
Whose words carry the shape of mountains
And the spirit of the Rio Grande.

Keresan, a bridge of bone and voice,
Horizon painted in the hues of survival,
Song only the land can sing
Only the heart can remember.

Keresan: The River That Speaks

It begins where the earth exhales,
Where cliffs hold their breath
Against the sky's vast glum gaze.

Keresan flows like obsidian rivers,
Shaping the tongue into a tool,
Not for words, but for the remembering
Of cornfields and fire circles,
Of rain pulling the sky down to touch land.

Each syllable is a seed,
Pressed deep into the soil of memory,
Roots pulling at the marrow of ancestors.
Vowels hold the curve of a potter's hand,
Consonants echo chant of canyons,
Pauses between them
Sacred as the spaces between stars.

In Santa Ana,
Keresan carries the weight of water,
Smooth and constant, carve the edges of the past.
In Acoma, it becomes the basalt cliffs
Stubborn, unyielding, immovable.
Every pueblo carries a note,
Together they sing the map of the cosmos.

To speak Keresan
Is to build the world again,
To call the spirits from the wind's spine,
To cup the land's face in your hands
And whisper its true name.

It is not a language.
Pulse of the Rio Grande,
Echo of mountains dreaming,
Ledger of stories written in firelight,

Read in the shadows of time.

To lose it would be to forget
How the sun folds itself into the horizon.
To let the song of the land
Slip back into silence.

Flames of the Desert

Beneath the unblinking sun of New Mexico,
The Zia rise with the fire of the red dawn,
Their four sacred directions painted
On the skin of the land
A sun symbol etched into eternity,
A compass of spirit and time.

Here, life is a circle,
Spinning in the rhythms of seasons,
Hands shaping clay into vessels
Carry not water,
But stories, prayers,
Weight of the cosmos itself.

Their dances
Not steps, but invocations
Summon rain from reluctant clouds,
Feet pressing into earth
Whispers into the ear of a god.

Across the mesa, the Cochiti
Carve their stories in stone,
Kiva walls murmur secrets
To those who know how to listen.
They are the makers of laughter,
Of clay storytellers
Whose mouths remain open
Spilling and unspilling the myths
Tethered to this land.

Every drumbeat an earthquake contained,
Vibration pulling the sky
Into their songs,
And the river listens,
Its waters bending at their call.

The Cochiti know that sound
Is not just heard but felt
Beneath the skin of the world.
Their masks hide not faces,
But the mysteries of creation,
Their dances paint invisible lines
On the canvas of the desert air.

The Zia stand with the sun,
Its rays a promise, a memory,
The Cochiti listen to earth's voice,
Echoes rippling through canyons.
Two flames, distinct, entwined,
Untwining, illuminate the story of a land
Still holding them both
A mother cradling her children
Unbroken, enduring, infinite.

Within the Concrete Forest

Beneath the towers of steel and glass,
The earth still hums with their presence.
The Haudenosaunee, People of the Longhouse,
Roots run deeper than the subway veins,
Stories older than the bricks that choke the soil.

In quiet pockets of forest and river,
The Onondaga tend to the sacred fire,
Its smoke a bridge between worlds,
Its warmth a reminder
That memory is not buried but planted,
Sprouting anew in each telling.

Wampum belts, woven from quahog shells,
Speak a language no skyscraper can silence
Every bead a thread
Binding treaties to generations,
Script etched in the language of tides.

Mohawks stand as the sharp edge of a blade,
Eyes fixed on horizons where storms gather,
A people who move with the wind,
Building bridges between worlds
With hands that reach for the heavens
And root deep in the earth,
Wielding steel like the branches of an ancient tree.

Mohawk ironworkers climb the city's skeleton,
Defy the dare of gravity with each step,
Hands gripping beams as if they were trees,
The skyline a forest to be tamed.
They carry the spirit of builders,
Constructing not skyscrapers and towers,
Bridges between what was and what remains.

In Seneca gatherings,

The cold air fills with the breath of flutes,
Their notes curling thick smoke
From the lips of ancient ceremonies.
The stomp dance shakes the ground,

Skilled feet drumming the earth awake,
Each movement a prayer
To the soil that remembers.

The rivers, Hudson, Mohawk, Susquehanna,
Whisper their names, carry essence in ripples,
Waters cradling the echoes of canoes,
Songs of fishing lines cast into memory.
And in the city's hidden places,
Yellow corn still grows,
Braided into husks of resistance.

Oneidas, with their hearts shaped like shields,
Guard the gates where history enters.
Quiet strength, carry weight of ancestors,
Arc of time bend in curve of prayers.
Silent thunder in a silent storm,
Steady beating heart in tight bodice of land.

Onondagas, keepers of the fire,
Wisdom as deep as the knowing forest floor,
Red roots weaving together in constant silence,
Smoke rising like a memory of forgotten stars.
Gather the winds of change,
Speaking in the language of cycles,
Wordless words are seeds planted
In the deep furrows of future generations.

Cayugas, tied to the water's edge,
Voices like ripples across the surface,
Stretching toward the horizon.
They listen to the song of fish,
Murmur of eternally running rivers
Carrying within them the ancient rhythm
Flow through the veins of pitted earth.

Senecas, rooted like the great oak,
Spirit like burly thunder splitting the sky.
In their hands, they shape the world,
Carving mountains and valleys, stones of time.
Heartbeat and echoes of the Confederacy,
Across tense war driven centuries,
Foundation built on wisdom,
Rock-strong as rocks beneath their feet.

Tuscaroras, arriving like gusts of wind at dusk,
Filling empty spaces with their song,
Novel new rhythms to the dance of Six Nations.
Steady steps leave footprints across the land,
The communal fire blazes high and bright,
Its embers a mosaic of ancient tongues,
Where humanity breathes, entwined
In the luminous strands of diversity.

The past hums, not as relic, but natural rhythm,
Beating softly, synchronically, beneath the stone,
Woven with winds that whisper and weave
Through shadowed alleys, sprawling open fields.
To tread these streets and pavements
Is to slip through the slippery veil of time,
To bear the weight of voices
Songs in tongues
That defy and splinter silence,
Refusing to fade or die. Singing in languages
That refuse refusal, to vanish.

The past is no relic; it drums, raw and feral,
Beneath cracked stone and asphalt veins,
Threads itself in gusts that claw
Through crooked alleys and barren plains.
New York, a murky, smoldering dream,
A land still haunted by its first rhythms,
The clans who called it home.

To walk these streets
Is to pierce the skin of centuries,
To carry the jagged weight of voices,
Traditions buried yet unbroken,
Like roots of ancient trees,
Hidden, alive,
Refusing to die.

Sacred Ice: Inuit Whispers in Alaska

Not conquerors,
But kin to the ice,
They carve their homes from breath and bone,
Sleds slicing tundra's unwritten histories.
Each crack in the frozen earth a whisper
Of seals, whales, the quiet generosity of the hunt.

The tundra stretching wide, earth meeting the sky,
Villages cradle icy shores, scattered stars.
Life bends to the rhythm of Arctic winds,
And the sea, a constant, feeds homes of the Iñupiat.

They do not flinch at winter's weight,
Their hands, like ancient tools,
Know the rhythm of carving, of sewing sinew,
Of summoning the spirit of a thing
Into its use.
They say, the blubber feeds more than hunger.
It feeds fire.
It feeds memory.

Seal breath rises through cracks in the ice;
The hunter waits, patient as time,
A harpoon clenched, the silence heavy with reverence.
Every creature claimed feeds not one, but all,
Bonds unbroken through endless winters.

Their stories are not written in books.
They are breathed out in the auroras,
Told with fingers tracing the shapes of ancestors
Along the stars' cold backs.
To sit beside them is to sit beside centuries,
Their words sharp as obsidian,
Shaping the contours of survival.

Ivory remembers the hands that carve,
Bone and stone echo stories of migrations,
Masks breathe life into ancestors' voices,
Dances trace paths of spirits unseen,
Binding the past and present with each gesture.

The bowhead's shadow moves beneath frozen seas,
Capture a prayer fulfilled, a life transformed.
Blubber fuels the lamps of long nights,
Bones shape tools, songs shape hearts,
As feasts erupt beneath sky's eternal gaze.

Stitched by hands that know the language of frost,
Fur wraps the body in its ancestral memory.
Seal gut whispers of rainproof resilience,
While sleds and tools, carved from bone and tusk,
Carry the weight of ancient wisdom into tomorrow.

The world is alive in every breath,
The spirit of seal, caribou, and whale speaks.
Rituals honor the unseen threads,
Connecting hunters to the earth, the ice, the stars,
A song that hums even as the shamans fade.

They read the ice as one reads a map,
Elders' voices echo in the young,
Teach the language of migrations and winds.
Survival dances between old and new,
Snowmobiles hum beside ancient chants.

Permafrost cradles the bounty of the hunt,
Meat dried to last through unyielding winters.
Cellars carved into frozen earth,
Where the season's abundance sleeps,
Wait, sustain life's fragile flame.

They walk with boots that echo sealskin's weight,
their shadows bending with the land's curve.
Where we see white endlessness,
they see pathways.

Where we see stillness,

they see the relentless hum of life
beneath the frostbitten surface.

The ice is thinner, its song fractured,
Homes built on permanence now tremble.
Tongues once fluent in Iñupiaq fall silent,
Yet the land remembers, the people endure,
Weaving new stories from the threads of the old.

Their art is not decoration.
It is prayer.
Ivory seals swim in miniature,
etched by hands guided by wind and instinct.
Masks with wide-open mouths howl
the songs of storms, ancestors, and spirits
all alive, all speaking,
all reminding them to listen.

This is not survival as the world thinks.
This is a pact,
made with the ice, the wind, the sea.
A promise to adapt,
to endure.

When the ice thins, they do not mourn it
like outsiders do.
They lean into the thinning,
knowing how to trace what remains,
how to live with it,
how to hold even a dying thing
with reverence.

Voices of the North: The Arctic and Subarctic: Between Ice and Fire

Voices of the Land: The First Nations of Canada

This land is not the dawn of a nation.
It is a river of many dawns,
Bone-deep, sky-woven, cedar-scented,
Etched with histories that rise from the soil,
Not planted upon it.

On the western edge of breath,
Where the wind sculpts totems out of cedar and song,
The Haida carve memory into the grain of the trees.
Each line is a story that ripples like tides,
Raven and Eagle watch the horizons
With eyes older than the sea.
Their canoes, like ocean's muscle,
Split the waters,
Bearing cedar masks
That whisper the language of transformation.
Here, even silence carries the weight of ancestors,
And the sky holds itself in deep reverence.

The Mohawk people walk the bridge of time,
Ironworkers strung between steel and sky
Builders of nations, carriers of sovereignty.
Once, they traced trails through endless forests,
The soul of the land beneath their moccasins,
Drumming in sync with the heartbeat of the deer.
They are keepers of the Great Law,
Their words braided like wampum
Each bead a covenant with the earth.
Their hands, scarred by history,
Still carry the fire of the Longhouse,
Where peace is a flame fed by long waiting.

In the rolling expanse of the prairies,
The Blackfoot ride the memory of the bison
Thunderous, unbroken herds
Clouds of muscle grazing the horizon.
They are hunters, dreamers,

Etching stories into buffalo hides
With red ochre and charcoal.
Their Sun Dance, a circle of life and blood,
Cries to the sky for renewal,
For the land's promise of abundance,
As the grasses whisper of treaties broken.

The Cree, a constellation strung across the north,
Their fires stars reflected in ice-covered rivers.
Hold the language of the forest in their tongues,
Its syntax rooted in birch bark,
Its verbs moving caribou-like through the Tundra.
Every word a ceremony,
A bond binding of human and nature
Mukluks brushing through snow,
Dreamcatchers gathering whispers
From spirits that wander the frost-stilled nights.

At the edge of the Atlantic,
Where the sea breathes its salt-laden hymns,
The Mi'kmaq weave ash and sweetgrass
Into baskets that hold the stories of ancestors.
Their hands remember the way of the waters,
Canoes slicing through mirrored faces of rivers.
The eel, the moose, the salmon,
These are not just prey but kin.
In the circle of their gathering,
The drum is a heartbeat
Echoing back the rhythm of the waves,
As the shore listens, quietly.

Where the mountains are cloaked in fog,
the Coast Salish people sing to the cedar forests.
Their longhouses rise like dreams from the earth,
Where smoke spirals skyward,
Calling spirits of ancestors to listen.
The salmon return to them as offerings,
A promise renewed each spring.
They paint the rivers with their songs,
The waters moving in time

With oars and stories passed down
Like drifting embers.

The Dene walk with the stars in their footsteps,
northern lights in the Northwest dancing above
Their prayers to the land and water.
Every river here is a vein of the earth,
Northern Alberta carries them in creak of snowshoes,
In the trembling songs of the drum.
The caribou's migration
Is a hymn they follow,
Its hooves shape the rhythm of survival.
To the Dene, the land breathes,
And the water remembers
Every ripple an echo of sacred balance.

On the shores of the Great Lakes,
The Huron-Wendat sowed fields of corn,
Watched by the eyes of crows and gods.
Farmers and traders, they built longhouses
of cedar and bark
Sanctuary of folktales and smoke.
They braided lives into the seasons,
Their spirits moving through the fields
With the wind's touch.
Each grain, each bead,
An offering to the earth,
A quiet pact of coexistence.

In the forests of Ontario and Quebec,
The Algonquin walk tender trails
As the trees keep secrets in their rings.
The rivers are their arteries,
Canoes slipping like whispers
Through mirror-still waters.
They speak the language of the loon's call,
The howl of wolves at dusk,
The rustle of leaves as the wind finds its voice.
Here, the forest is not a refuge;

It is the world entire
Each branch a map,
Each stream a story waiting to unfold.

Beneath the stretch of northern skies,
The Ojibwe's spirit moves with the wind,
Where the lakes of Ontario mirror the vastness,
And the boreal forest hums with ancient voices.
By the shores of Wabigoon, they gather,
Offering prayers with cedar smoke rising,
Their birchbark canoes cutting through the water,
They paddle through their waking dreams,
In the stillness of night, the drumbeat echoes,
A rhythm that carries the weight of generations,
The heart of the Anishinaabe alive and enduring.

Where the Yukon river carves its path,
The Tlingit gather beneath cedar coastal beams,
Stories held in the curve of a carved totem.
Cedar smoke drifts through the village,
Elders trace clan crests on carved totems,
The eyes of Raven and Wolf watching.
In the great cedar house, drums speak in steady beats,
Against the mountains, voices rising like the tide,
As dancers move, wrapped in woven Chilkat robes,
And the past comes alive in every step.

In the cedar halls, Raven and Eagle stand apart,
mirroring each other in the currents of time.
Their stories carve paths through ancient trees,
winding down to waters where salmon rise
echoes from forgotten moments.
Each clan holds its breath in the weave of a basket,
the carved face of an ancestor catching the light.
In the rhythm of the tides, in the silence of the mountains,
the Tlingit speak without asking
from the land, the sea, the bones of the earth,
passing through generations like a song that never fades.

On the open plains of Saskatchewan and Manitoba,
Where the grass bends with the wind's breath,
The Dakota and Nakoda ride beneath endless skies,
Hooves drum against the earth like an ancient song.
Tipis rise in a circle, the fire at their heart,
Smoke curling toward the spirits.
Elders pass the pipe, voices low, as
Stories flow like rivers through generations.

Along the Wolastoq River, where mist rises at dawn,
The Maliseet move in the rhythm of the water.
Canoes gliding through the current,
Wooden frames hold the memory of many hands.
In the wigwams, elders weave stories into ash-splint baskets,
The drum's steady beat carries the voices of ancestors.
The river is not just water.
It is the breath of the land,
The path that has always led them home.

In the shadow of the Chilcotin Plateau,
Where rivers cut deep into the earth,
The Tsilhqot'in ride across open grasslands,
Horses moving as if guided by the wind.
The smell of dried salmon lingers in the air,
Woven into cedar shelters where elders gather.
In the winter lodges, they carve and paint,
Stories unfold in the curve of antlers and wood.
The land listens, holds the weight of their ancestors' steps.

First Nations voices rise like smoke,
Spiral against the forgetting winds.
Their lands, their waters, their skies,
These are not histories to be erased,
But continuities carved into the present.
The trees bend to their songs,
The rivers carry their stories.
And even now,
In the quiet persistence of their traditions,
They remain the land's first true guardians.

Blood of Two Rivers

Wind moves through the tall prairie grass,
Whispering stories carried in both French and Cree,
In the cadence of a Red River fiddle,
In the measured steps of a jig that shakes the dust.

The Métis do not vanish.
They rise with the sun over the Prairies,
Their steps light upon the soil, yet unshakable,
Like the fiddler's bow drawn across the strings,
Like the fire that never dies.

They are the people of the road,
Born of voyageurs and First Nations,
Raised on the curve of the river,
Where buffalo once darkened the horizon.
Not settlers, not wholly native
Something new, something strong,
Woven from two worlds, yet claimed by neither,
Who stitched buffalo hide into moccasins,
And know the weight of a musket in their hands.

Red River runs thick with memory,
Ox carts creaking under endless sky,
Hooves pressing deep into the land,
Mapping a history that refuses to fade.
The carts carried more than furs and pemmican
They bore names unrecorded,
Promises unfulfilled,
A people who would not be written out.

They speak in the language of voyageurs,
Their words shaped by the rivers they paddled,
By the compulsion of the hunt,
The smell of pemmican drying in the sun.
They know the touch of sinew on leather,
The curve of a bow,
The sharp weight of iron traps,
The way frost settles into the bones
After a night beneath the northern lights.

A sash tightens around the waist,
Crimson threads woven with restraint,
Every fiber a story
Of the ones who refused to vanish,
Of a nation declared illegal,

Of land taken and names erased,
But never the spirit.
The sash holds more than fabric;
It binds generations,
It carries the strength of hands
That fought, that built, that endured.

The earth remembers the Métis step,
Light upon the soil, yet unshakable,
Like the fiddler's bow drawn across strings,
Like the fire that never dies.

They remember Batoche,
Where bullets tore through the willows,
Where voices rose in defiance
Before they were drowned in gunfire.
Louis Riel stands in the shadow of history,
His words still burning in the wind:
"Our people will sleep for one hundred years,
But when they awake, it will be the artists
Who give them back their spirit."

The land remembers them,
The rivers hum their names,
The wind carries their songs forward
Not past, not lost,
But living.

Wind moves through the tall prairie grass
It does not carry whispers; it carries footsteps,
A thousand migrations pressed into the soil,
Names that never made it into history books,
Words spoken in tongues that colonizers
Could not twist into treaties.Métis. People of the road.
Not settlers. Not First Nations.

Something else. Something untamed.
Born of voyageurs who drank the sky in tin cups,
Of Cree women who traced rivers with their hands,
Who held the knowledge of land in their bones
Long before maps carved it into submission.

The Red River is not just water.
It is blood, it is history unravelin
In ox-cart tracks, in musket fire,
In the scent of pemmican drying under an unblinking sun.

The wheels groan over frozen ground,
Their rhythm like the pulse of a people
Who refuse to be erased.

They wear their history in the threads of a sash
Red like rebellion, blue like stolen land,
Gold like the flicker of firelight on caribou hide.
They dance to a fiddle that does not forget,
Feet pounding dust into memory,
Shaking loose the silence
Forced upon them by laws and guns.

They remember Batoche.
Not as a story, not as ink on paper
but as a wound that never fully closes.
Louis Riel, standing at the crossroads of time,
Watching his people wake from a century of sleep,
His voice still burning in the wind:
My people will sleep for one hundred years,
but when they awake,
it will be the artists who give them back their spirit.

Métis do not vanish.
They rise with the frost in the morning,
They move with the rivers,
They burn like the Northern Lights,
Brief, brilliant, uncontainable.

The land does not forget them.
Neither should history.

Arctic Breath of the Inuit

In the frozen edges of the world,
The sky wears its stars like ancient beads,
They walk, their steps sharp as breath of wolves.
They carve their songs from the ice,
Sounds of ancestors curling beneath the ground,
Waiting for the light to crack open the day.

In the heart of the northern dusk,
Where the wind speaks in ancient tongues,
They build homes of snow,
Igloos rising like the breath of a sleeping bear,
Soft arcs of white,
Shelter them from silence, the world outside.
Inside, the warmth hums like a heartbeat,
The walls thick with stories,
Each block of ice a memory,
Each curve a passage back
to the earth they have always known.
Their fires glow like distant stars
Steady, unyielding, the flame, a symbol
Against a world that is constantly on the edge of freezing.

The sea, a slow-moving canvas,
Paints their existence in shades of grey and blue.
Their canoes, built from bones and skin,
Cuts through water seal-graceful,
Slipping into the quiet depths.
They hunt with knives honed by centuries,
Sharp blades slicing through the quiet of the ice,
Whale, seal, and walrus offering themselves
To the rhythm of need,
Unspoken covenant between land and people.
Every breath of the hunt sacred,
Woven into, pact not broken by time,
Made eternal in the stretch of the sky.

The Inuit speak a language of the land,
Not words, but the of the world itself.

Syllables roll the wind across the Tundra,
Layered with the meaning of meaning,
Every sound a landscape,
A rock, a river,
A storm.
Inuktitut, the tongue of ice and light,

Speaks of the world they know,
Not with names, but with gestures,
With the call of the raven in the distance,
With the glint of snow under the midnight sun.
It does not need to describe what is seen,
It embodies what is felt,
What is known in quiet spaces between breaths.
They speak not in sentences, but in moments,
In the weight of the sky on their shoulders,
Sound of a sled moving across fresh snow,
Echo of an animal's call through the vast emptiness.

In the vast silence of the Arctic,
Earth humming beneath layers of frost,
The Inuvialuit trace paths like cracked ice,
Their journey marked by rhythm of winds
That crackle like ancient firewood.
Nunavummiut step across the snow,
Leave footprints shift, moon's reflection
On a frozen lake,
Where the sky holds its breath.
Nunatsiavut Inuit, of the north, their
Hearts beating with the tides of the sea,
Their songs carried by the salt and the snow.
The Nunavik Inuit, sculptors of the cold,
Live in the breath of the storm,
Jagged peaks of mountains rising
Silent witnesses of time's passage.

In their heart lies the rhythm of the hunt,
Unspoken bond between earth and spirit.
Their elders, like living archives,
Carry the history of their people in their bones,

Memories, sharp knives to carve the whale's flesh,
Steady as the ice that holds the world in place.
Teach their young not only how to survive,
but how to listen to the land,
How to hear the tale spun in breaking of ice,
In the rise of the northern lights,
In the howl of the wind that shapes their path.
Each tale woven from fabric, passed down
In gestures, in dreams,
In the rhythm of life that beats like a drum
Beneath the surface of the earth.

They gather in their homes,

In the stillness of the Arctic night,
Where the wind howls like a forgotten song,
Where the stars speak in a language older than time.
The fire flickers,
Its light casting long shadows on the walls,
As the elders speak of the spirits of animals,
Of the ghosts of ancestors living in the wind,
In the ocean,
In the ice.
The children listen, their eyes wide,
Hearing the ancient rhythms of their people,
Hearing the pull of the land
That will never let them go.
They learn the ways of the snow,
How to read the sky,
How to understand the whispers of the world
That only the Inuit can hear.

Their homes are not just shelter
They are places where stories breathe,
Where language speaks,
Where the cold is both enemy and companion,
Where the warmth of their fire
Is a defiance of the world's harshness.
The world outside freezes,
But inside, the air is full of life,

Full of memory,
Full of those who have lived and loved
Hunted beneath the vast, endless sky.

When the night falls and the winds rise,
They pull their furs tighter around them,
Gathering warmth of a thousand lifetimes,
Watch the stars trace paths across heavens,
Silent, steady,
The eternal witnesses to all that is.

This is their world:
Not a place,
But a beat that never falters,
As old as the earth beneath their feet.

The Ones Who Walk with Reindeer

Wind slashes the tundra,
a knife against flesh,
but the old hands know the stitch,
how to mend sky with sinew,
how to read the hunger of snow.

The reindeer move muscle and bone,
their breath vanishing before learning the air.
A thousand hooves drum
against ice that forgets nothing.

They have walked this whiteness
for a thousand years,
descendants of voices woven in fur and frost,
their name - n'enyts
not a mark of land,
but of being.

The chum rises where the land allows,
its reindeer-hide walls
holding the weight of winter,
stitched against the wind's sharp teeth.
It folds, unfolds,
moves as they do
never rooted, never lost.

Fur-lined hands fasten *yagushka* seams,
the thick warmth of reindeer hide
layered with quiet patience of survival.
Embroidered patterns whisper of
ancestors who sewed the cold away,
who walked beneath the same merciless sky
and made it theirs.

The river listens.
The wind carries voices
from those who have gone before.
The shaman kneels,
presses his palms to the frozen earth,

listens for the pulse beneath.
Firelight flickers across his face
a language older than words,
older than time.

Here, where the land does not end
but simply gives way to wind,
they fasten their tents against permafrost,
read the sky's shifting moods,
thread their days through Yamal's open hands
the end of the land,
the beginning of all that matters.

The child's fingers trace
her father's fur-lined hood,
stories of blizzards pressed into his skin.
The past walks beside them,
pulling the sled,
wrapping its arms around the fire's weak light.

In the cities, voices speak in broken tongues,
laws carve fences where none should be,
but the Nenets walk,
step after step,
across a land that does not belong
because it never had to.

Nomads of the tundra moving with herds,
guiding reindeer through shifting seasons,
across rivers turned to glass, over earth
that never sleeps, their steps marked
by instinct, not by maps. A thousand kilometers,
the land stretches and calls,
and they follow, as they always have.

At the Russian Nenets reindeer festival,
the past stands tall, racing hooves beat to
rhythms older than empires, voices rise
in chants that name the winds, hands grip sleds,
muscles test the frost, they gather, not just
to compete, but to remember, to weave
another year into the story of their kind.

But the ice thins, the seasons falter,
permafrost softens under heavy hooves,

storms rise where stillness once ruled,
rivers swell, then vanish too soon.
The land shifts in ways no elders recall,
and the herds must learn new paths, or be lost.

Pipelines carve through sacred ground,
steel and smoke replace the open sky.
The Nenets watch as roads divide,
as drills hum where silence once spoke.
Gas and oil, wealth for some,
for them, another way of life at risk.

The Breath of Sápmi

Beneath the endless arcs of the northern sky,
Sámi tread land woven with bones of their ancestors.
Here, the earth speaks in whispers,
not words,
but a language older than the cold winds.
The wind, too, knows their names,
how they are written in the language of the birch trees,
how they are carried in the breath of the reindeer.

Through the vast stretches of Sápmi -
Norway, Sweden, Finland, Russia,
a single thread ties the heartbeats together.
In the unbroken silence of the tundra,
their voices rise,
sung in tongues that tremble with the weight of centuries,
though some are now shadows,
fading in the mouths of the young.

They are the keepers of the herds,
the ones who move like shadows,
whispers on the wind,
under the pulse of midnight sun and the silver moon.
Reindeer stride through their bloodline,
skimming over the snow like silent ships
bound for some unknown horizon.

A slow, steady hum rises from the earth,
a song without beginning or end.
The joik echoes in the cold air,
a call to the mountains, to the waters,
to the bones of their people—
a memory pressed into the shape of a song
that lingers like the taste of salt.

And still, they endure.
Not by forgetting
but by remembering the earth's promise

the way it returns,
season by season,
long after the weight of history
has pressed its footprints into their skin.
The Sámi hold fast to what remains
and to what can never be taken:
the language of the land,
the touch of the snow,
the strength of the herd,
the wisdom of those who speak
in the silence of the night.

And though the world turns,
sweeping away all but the bones,
they remain,
the Sámi
carrying the ancient pulse,
the voices of the earth,
the wind and the snow,
alive in every step they take.

The *gákti* drapes them like a second skin,
colors drawn from the earth's own palette,
reds like flames dancing at the edge of the world,
blues that mirror the depth of midnight lakes,
yellow like the first light of dawn on frozen ground.
Each thread tells a story,
a family marked by the design of the collar,
a village echoed in the curve of the sleeve.
They wear their history in patterns,
woven by hands that have known the land
for millennia, the wool and leather carry the weight
of a thousand lives, the beadwork like starlight
tracing their steps across the snow.

The *joik* rises from the heart,
not bound by the form of words,
but by that beating between soul and the earth.
It is the call of the mountain,
the echo of the lake,
the wind's sigh,

the cry of the reindeer in the night.
Each note a thread,
each breath a part of the landscape,
as voices rise and fold into the cold air,
swelling like a storm,
softening like the snow falling in silence.
They do not sing *of* the land; they sing it,
until it becomes the song and the song becomes them.

The *joik* is not meant for the ear alone,
but for the body,
for the pulse of the land in the blood.
It can hold grief in its trembling highs,
or joy in its low hums,
it can touch the soul of a stranger
and pull it deep into the world of the Sámi,
where every person, every stone,
every wind has its own song to sing.
It is the music of the land that cannot be forgotten,
the rhythm of existence,
held in the spaces between breaths,
in the heartbeats of those who still know how to listen.

The earth, the sun, the moon,
they are not separate from the Sámi,
but partners,
woven together like threads in an endless tapestry.
The rivers hum with ancient wisdom,
the rocks are voices waiting to be heard.
Spirits live in the birch trees,
in the northern lights that flicker like the pulse of a beating heart,
in the reindeer that roam, free,
in the spirits of the ancestors who never left.

In the face of the winds of change,
the Sámi rise again,
no longer silent,

but speaking in their own tongues,
carrying their banners in chambers of parliaments,

through the courts,
across the lands where their forebears walked.
They speak not only for themselves,
but for the earth,
for the rivers that run too swiftly to be silenced,
for the mountains that stand unmoving,
for the snow that covers the ground in silence.
Their voice is rising,
gathering strength from the land,
as they claim back what was always theirs.

The People Who Speak the Land

The wind knows their name before it is spoken.
It carries syllables of Yup'ik, soft as salmon bones,
Rolls the weight of Siberian Yupik over the frozen tide,
Whispers Naukan Yupik to the cliffs that still listen.

They are the ones who carve history into ice,
Read the flight of the ptarmigan like scripture.
Before steel ships came, before borders divided sea,
They moved as the seal moves, as the
Walrus knows where the ice will break.

Here, where the Bering fog thickens into myth,
Where the sun hovers and refuses to set,
They follow the old songs, the ones stitched
Into skin boats, into the rhythm of the oar,
Into the hands that lift the harpoon
With knowledge older than the maps
That do not know their names.

Houses half-buried, warm as an animal's den,
Fires coaxing marrow from the bones of winter,
Elders threading stories through cracks of time,
Outside, the cold gnaws at the edges of memory.
They have lived where no one else dared to,
Speaking to the land in a tongue it remembers,
Though it has forgotten so many.

The land does not give freely,
it must be known, courted, respected.
They take what is needed—no more.
A seal, its breath still warm, its spirit
sent back into the deep with whispered thanks.
A whale, its ribs rising like cathedral beams
as they carve life from its vast body,
knowing the debt is never paid in full.

Their homes crouch low against the wind,
Qasgiq where men gather in the dark months,
Learning the slow patience of the hunt,
Enet where families press close,
Heat rising from the earth itself.
In summer, skins stretch over wooden frames,
Temporary as footprints on the shore.

The drum does not forget.
It speaks in the hollow of the chest,
Calls ancestors from the marrow of the tundra,
Wakes the old spirits sleeping in the rivers.
The shaman walks between the worlds,
Bone and breath, water and fire,
Speaking with the wind, calling
The names the ice still remembers.

The stories do not end.
They are held in the hands that sew sinew,
In the feet that dance over frozen ground,
In the tongues that refuse to go silent.
Even now, when the world calls them past,
When ice thins and voices fade,
They remain.
A people who speak the land.

The river does not freeze as it once did.
The ice pulls away too soon,
The fish do not return in the same numbers.
The old words are slipping,
Torn between satellite signals and fading echoes.
Children learn both tongues but dream in only one.
The village store replaces the hunt,
Plastic and metal where bone and sinew once held.
The world leans in, heavy, relentless,
But they stand between past and present,
between land and machine,
between what was and what must remain.

Chukchi: Bone, Ice, and Breath

They move where the reindeer move,
hooves drumming the old rhythm
into a land that does not listen,
eyes tracing the constellations
etched into night before the first words were spoken.
Their hands, weathered by wind,
fasten rawhide, guide the sled,
press against the warm flank of an animal
that knows no shelter but them.

Their tongues cut the air like blades
Chukchi language, thick with wind and hunger,
with the weight of the dead and the wisdom of those
who never left.
Russian creeps in, tries to settle in their mouths,
but their syllables twist against it,
like ice refusing to melt in the wrong season.

The Soviet wind came like a blizzard,
It cut across the bones of the land,
leaving footprints where there were none.
It told them their gods were false,
their songs were of no consequence.
In the dark, the reindeer were driven into pens,
and the sky was folded under a banner,
erasing the sacred names of places
and the spirits that dwelled in them.
They were told to forget,
but the forgetting never took.
The earth held their hearts in its frozen grip,
and beneath the weight of history,
they found, once again,
the ember of their ancestors' fire.

The spirits are not distant.
They are in the breath of the wind,
in the crackle of fire,
in the press of the reindeer's hooves

against the frozen earth.
The shaman's voice rises like smoke,
dancing on the edge of a storm,
calling upon the spirits of the land,
the ones who have never left
and the ones who will never return.
They listen with ears open to the sky,
seeking answers in the rustle of leaves
or the silence of the snow.

Memory lives in their hands
carving tusk and bone into shapes
that do not shatter, do not vanish.
A walrus, a spirit, a dream
something to outlast the long dark.
The stories are told in firelight,
shadows moving against walls of the world,
a voice rising like a gull's cry over the black water,
reminding the ice that they are still here.

The tundra does not forgive
it does not cradle, does not console.
It stretches, white and infinite,
a frozen lung that exhales no warmth,
a body that has never known softness.

The sea is not a refuge
it is a beast, ancient and unchained,
its mouth swallowing the horizon,
its back breaking beneath the weight of storms.
The ice cracks like ribs in winter,
splitting open to reveal the black depths
where no mercy sleeps.

And yet, they remain.

They do not own the cold.
They carve it.
They harness it.
They make it carry their name.

The Sea's Quiet Witness

The Aleut, the Unangan,
Whisper the sea's name in a tongue shaped by wind,
where every word stirs the salt of ancient shores.
Not of stone and fire, but of water and sky
they speak the rhythm of tides,
the voice of the ocean's breath
a language born of salt,
carved into each syllable,
each wave a verse they inherit.

Beneath their hands,
the land offers its bones:
ivory, whale, and wood,
fashioned into tools,
refined over centuries of ice and storm.
Each stone smoothed by the edges of necessity,
each knot of sinew woven
from knowledge passed through generations
of eyes that have watched the endless horizon,
of hearts that know the silence before the hunt.

The Aleut live in the space between
the world of the visible and the unseen,
where the sea gathers the stories of ancestors
and whispers them back
in the creak of a kayak
that rides the rhythm of the tides.

No garden grows here,
no sacred grove of trees,
but beneath the surface,
the kelp forests wave their limbs
in quiet reverence.
The earth itself offers its abundance,
from seals to sea birds,
from roots wrapped in frost
to berries hidden beneath thick moss.

Their eyes are sharp as the cliffs,

their feet sure on the ice,
tracking in silence the rhythm of life
that has always been,
will always be.

They came from across the sea,
with promises of new worlds,
but their words were heavy with fire,
their eyes full of greed.

Aleut, folded into the grip of foreign hands
hands that spread disease like shadows
across the land they knew,
taking not only bodies but time itself,
stitching threads of pain into fabric of memory.
The land became a place of sorrow,
of forced labor and broken spirits,
fur trade silenced old ways
and shifted the tides of a culture
flowed freely for centuries.

Yet the sea never left them.
In the silence of the storm,
their voices persisted,
quiet but strong,
woven through the art they still carry:
the delicate twists of baskets,
the patterns etched in bone and ivory,
each line a story,
each curve a tribute to a past
that refuses to fade.
Their hands still carve the spirit of land
into the tools they use to survive,
to hunt, to remember.

Today, they walk in two worlds.
The hum of engines replaces the thrum of paddles,
but the sea still calls them,

still holds them close,
as their ancestors were held
in the folds of a kayak,
the sharp scent of salt on the air.
Modernity mixes with memory,
and the Aleut remember who they are:
the ones who survived the tides,
who built their homes from whale bone
and hope. They speak in the old tongue,
and in the language of the world today,
words that stretch from one shore to next,
one story to the other.

Through the Canopy: Indigenous Voices
of ... and Central America

Through the Canopy: Indigenous Voices
of South and Central America

The Ancient Souls of the Arawak

The Arawaks were woven into the land,
Each step a silent echo of the earth they touched,
Rivers ran like threads through their lives,
Silent as the moon that knew their faces,
Spanning the Bahamas, the shores of Hispaniola,
Where the mountains stand as ancestors,
Breathing stories into the air,
Where the breeze curls the skin of the earth
And palms carry memories of rituals unseen.

Beneath the sun's unyielding gaze,
They emerged from the earth's breath,
Their footsteps tracing the contours of islands
That rose like broken teeth from the sea.
The Arawak, people of cassava and fire,
People of the bohío and the caney,
Their hands shaping clay into vessels
That held the stories of rivers and storms.
The Taíno bent the earth to their hands,
Raised cassava from the patient soil,
Mounded the land in spirals and circles,
A sacred geometry of survival.
With coa sticks, carving life into the island,
Harvesting the marrow of the earth,
Feeding generations with roots that never forgot.

In the Greater Antilles, building villages
Where the air hummed with songs of ancestors,
Where the zemis watched from carved wood,
Their eyes holding the weight of the sky.
The Taíno, their voices rising like smoke,
Called to Yúcahu, god of the sea,
And Atabey, mother of fresh waters,
Prayers woven into the roots of ceiba trees.
Knowing the language of hurricanes,
The rhythm of tides,

The secrets of yuca buried deep in the soil.
Their canoes cut through waves,
Carrying the weight of trade and kinship,
Connecting islands like threads in a net.

When the first ship darkened the horizon,
A thousand years of light dimmed in a breath,
The world twisted, a crack in the earth's bones
As men with iron hearts and shining promises
Laid siege to the lives that had always been,
Made islands into prisons,
Sent songs into silence, carved marks
Into faces where names once stood proud.

The bohío stood at the heart of the village,
Round and warm, cradling breath and laughter,
While the caney watched over the people,
A house for the chiefs,
A place where memory and wisdom sat unshaken,
Even when the storm rose beyond the reefs.

At night, the zemis whispered in the dark,
Carved from wood, from stone, from bone,
Their hollow eyes holding the wind's song,
Their bodies small, yet vast as the sky.
The Taíno danced, feet pressing offerings into the dust,
Singing to the spirits that wove the world,
To the rain, the fire, the unseen hands that
Shaped the island long before men arrived in sails.

Then came the hunger of foreign hands,
The whip against skin that had only known sun,
Bodies bent beneath the weight of gold
That would never be theirs.
The rivers ran red where only fish had swum,
Smoke replaced the breath of the bohíos,
And the children who once chased the sea
Were swallowed by fever, by chains, by silence.
Yet the earth remembers.

Cuba, Jamaica, Haiti - names carried like seeds,
Scattered across waters that whisper their words.
In the veins of those who remain,
The Lokono, the tongues that refuse to still,
The stories told in firelight, in wood, in drumbeats,
The Arawak live, not as ghosts,
But as roots deep beneath the soil,
Waiting for the wind to call them home.

In their voices, the wood sang,
An intimate language, unbroken
By the sharp, foreign tongues
That tore the horizon wide with promises
Of gold, of God, of glory.
But there were no new gods in their hearts,
Only the sun, the tides, and the stars.
Only their hands shaping canoes from
The belly of the forest, carrying them across
The restless water to meet their kin
Beneath the shadow of a jagged sky.

But their stories,
Unwritten on fragile paper,
Still curl at the edges of the wind,
Hold steady in the eyes of those
Who remember the way the earth tastes untouched,
The weight of the sky when you trust the storm,
And how the bones of the past
Still walk the beach at dusk,
Among the broken shells,
Among the ancient echoes
That refuse to be erased.

Yanomami

The river does not forget the hands that cup its water,
nor the feet that press into its muddy veins.
The forest listens, breathes, folds
Its green arms around those who know its oldest names.

Here, where the mist moves like whispered stories,
the Yanomami walk, not as strangers,
but as the soul beneath the bark,
the hush between leaf and rain.

Gold-seekers come, their hands heavy with hunger,
their machines chewing into the ribs of the earth.
They call it progress,
but the spirits scream in the poisoned streams,
and the children cough with lungs full of ghosts.

The shamans still dream,
still call the spirits of jaguar and storm,
still paint their bodies with the language of the unseen.
But the sky has changed.
The air tastes of something forgotten, something stolen.

Who will listen when the forest falls silent?
Who will carry the stories when the last root is severed?

The Yanomami know,
it is not the jungle that needs them,
it is the world.

Mapuche: We Who Do Not Bow

The wind does not ask permission to move,
nor do we.
We are the ones who did not kneel before the Inca,
who watched their golden empire halt at our rivers,
who sent their armies retreating into the thin air of their own mountains.

Then came the ones with iron skin,
men who carried crosses but no prayers,
whose hunger smelled of rust and burning flesh.
They named us savage
because we would not be broken,
because our bodies did not fit their chains.

Three hundred years we held the line.
Three hundred years we spoke in fire,
stained the soil with the weight of their horses,
turned forests into fortresses,
woven shields of leather and will.
Lautaro rode like the wind -
our warrior, our strategist, our spear of resistance.
They took him, but not his shadow.
It still moves through the Araucanía,
whispering in the tall grasses,
waiting.

And now, they build roads over our bones,
call our rivers government property,
slice the Mapu into deeds and fences,
as if the earth belongs to ink and paper.
They say history is past,
but history does not sleep.
It breathes in the hands of the weaver,
the *kultrun*'s steady drumbeat,
the *machi's* prayers rising with the smoke of the *lawen*.

We do not ask for what is already ours.
The land remembers.
The rivers speak our names.
And the wind,
the wind still does not ask permission to move.

But the war never ended.
They came with flags instead of swords,
with treaties written in vanishing ink,
with machines that cut forests down to their roots,
digging deep into the bones of our ancestors.
They called it pacification, conquest,
we call it theft.

Still, we rise.
We reclaim what was never theirs to take.
We stand where the trees once stood,
where rivers choke on industry's waste,
where the land remembers
and refuses to forget.
We are the fire they could not drown,
the voices they could not silence.
Mapuche, still standing.
Mapuche, still the land.

They tried to unmake our tongue,
to press it into the corners of silence,
to drown it beneath the weight of language.
But Mapudungun is the voice of the land,
the whisper of rain on the pewen's leaves,
the breath of wind shaping the mountains.
It does not die.
It moves between our lips,
carried in the songs of the elders,
woven into the stories that refuse to be forgotten.
We speak, and the land listens.

Our hands remember what the earth taught them.
The loom sings as we weave,

thread by thread,
stories pressed into fabric,
geometries of sky and river,
the memory of the land made visible.
Our silver catches the light,
moon-metal shaped into symbols of lineage,
a history that rests against our chests,
in the curve of an earring,
in the weight of the *trapelacucha*,
a reminder that we are not unadorned,
that we have never been invisible.

And when the drum speaks,
the world listens.
The *kultrun* carries the heartbeat of the *Mapu*,
its skin stretched tight with history,
its rhythm calling us back to the center,
where the dance moves in circles,
where the past and the future meet,
where we rise,
where we rise,
where we rise.

Quechua: The Stone and the Sky

You did not vanish.
Inca empire fell, but you did not.
Your tongue still wraps the wind,
your hands still carve the mountains.
The Andes remember your footprints,
pressed deep into the spine of the world,
where silver veins bled for strangers
but never broke your spirit.

Ecuador, Bolivia, Peru,
your words rise with the mist,
curl through market stalls in Cusco,
echo in the salt flats of Uyuni,
linger in the highland winds of Quito.
Chile, Argentina, Colombia,
your tongue weaves through borders,
carried in the breath of elders,
rooted in the earth,
unyielding as the Andes themselves.

Before Inca empire, there were voices,
Wari stone, Tiwanaku sun,
hands etching history into the highlands.
Quechua walked these valleys
Long before crowns of gold
and roads of conquest.
Then came Inca empire, rising like breath
Tawantinsuyu, vast as the sky,
held together not by swords,
but by syllables carried on the wind.
Quechua, the thread through mountains,
binding cities, rivers, and time itself.

Spaniards came with iron and hunger,
with crosses that burned names into the earth,
with laws that bent the spine,
with tongues that unmade histories.

But Quechua did not break.
It hid in the hush of mountain passes,
slipped between rosary prayers,
clung to the lullabies of mothers
who whispered the old world into the new.

Now, it rises again
on radio waves, in classrooms,
in the mouths of poets and farmers,
in breath of those who refuse to be forgotten.
Speaking in hushed syllables of rivers,
in songs woven into alpaca wool,
in fields where potatoes sleep
under the watchful eye of the condor.
Quechua drifts through circuits and screens,
etched into fiber optics,
woven into beats that shake the earth.

A young voice sings to the ancestors
in a language they feared would fade,
carving new paths where old echoes remain.
Hands that built the terraces still shape
the land, fingers pressing seeds into soil,
spinning stories into cloth, tying
the past to the present with every thread.
Pachamama listens as the loom speaks, as feet
strike the ground in rhythms older than empire.

Quechua, you are the voice of the old gods,
the sun's children,
the keepers of coca and fire,
whispering to Pachamama
as she listens, always,
always.
They told you time was linear,
but you knew better.
Past and present walk side by side,
one foot in the golden city,
one foot in the soil.

The Glyphs Remember

The Mayans carved language from stone,
breath pressed into rock, into bark, into clay,
a world woven in glyphs, each curve of the hand a word,
each word a memory.
They wrote time, they wrote blood,
they wrote the gods into being.
The flames came later, Spanish hands unmaking centuries,
ash rising where jaguars once prowled
the margins of the codices.
But the glyphs remember, buried in the bones of the temples,
whispering in the wind that moves through ruins.

In the hush of the jungle, zero was born
not absence, but breath. Silent pause between heartbeats,
the shape of the cycle before it begins again.
They counted the sky, measured the tilt of the earth,
knew the weight of time before the world understood
the vastness of numbers etched in stone and stars.

They read the night with unerring eyes,
traced fire across the sky,
spun time in interlocking wheels.
The Haab' marked the rhythm of corn and rain,
the Tzolk'in whispered the voice of the gods,
the Long Count stretched into eternity,
measuring the rise and fall of empires.
Stone and sky, shadow and sun,
their calendars turned like breathing,
never forgetting the shape of the universe.

Stone rises from the jungle, not ruins,
but echoes of an empire that still breathes.
Tikal's pyramids reach beyond the canopy,
Chichen Itza's steps summon serpent to dance with the light.

Palenque, where kings sleep beneath carved vaults, Copán,
where the stairways speak in the language of stone time.
Not tombs, not relics, not memories turned to dust.
Thresholds, waiting for footsteps to wake them again.

They saw divinity in stone and clay,
in jade shaped like sacred faces,
in woven threads that caught the sun.
They painted the world in blood-red and deep ochre,
scribed stories on walls that never forgot.
Bonampak sings in the dark, the colors still vivid,
battle cries and ritual chants frozen
in pigments that refuse to fade.
The gods still live in these hands,
in the lines of a sculptor's touch,
in the stories that will not be silenced.

In the dense heart of Mesoamerica,
where the ceiba tree roots into earth and sky,
the Maya emerged, shaping the land with temples
of limestone and calendars of time.
Stone cities rose, not as one empire, but as
constellations, each a sovereign light,
Tikal's towering ambition, Palenque's delicate inscriptions,
Copán's intricate glyphs whispering to the gods.
Chichen's space, Calakmul's power, a rival's throne.

Across centuries, the jungle held their footsteps,
echoing with chants of maize and sacrifice,
the mathematics of the cosmos etched into temple walls.
Trade wove the lowlands and highlands together
jade, obsidian, cacao flowing like rivers of influence.

Then, silence crept in. Cities
emptied, their causeways swallowed by vines.
Was it the ancient skies that betrayed them,
sealing the rains behind a curtain of drought?

Or war, a slow unraveling of power?
The end was not an end. Their spirit pressed forward,
through new towns, shifting tides, changing gods.
The classic collapse, a mystery profound. Droughts,
wars, or gods? The truth lies somewhere in between.

Even as Spanish steel carved its shadow,
the Maya endured in languages still spoken,
in hands that weave the past into the present.
The jungle may have reclaimed the temples,
but the people remain,
their history rooted deeper than stone.

Nomads, Shamans, and First Peoples: Asia's Indigenous Heritage

Adivasis

The forest does not need a name.
It was here before names.
Before Jharkhand was Jharkhand,
before Chhattisgarh was carved from rock,
before borders and deeds and maps,
the Gonds, the Santhals, the Bhils,
walked paths of *mahua* and *sal*,
their feet writing histories into the soil.

They move like wind threading bamboo groves,
their language unbound by weight of scripts,
each syllable a river bending through time,
unwritten, carved into earth's remembering.
The Nagas, Mizos, Khasis, mountain echoes,
feet steady on shifting clouds,
drums beating beneath the skin of the night,
history not archived, not sung, but danced.

The trees remember.
The rivers hold the songs
of hands grinding millet on stone,
of women weaving bamboo into shelter,
of gods who do not sit in temples
but live in the fire and the hunt,
in the whisper of leaves before the monsoon.

They say land belongs to the one who fences it,
to the one who writes its worth in numbers.
But whose hands lifted the first grain from the earth?
Whose children knew the taste of fruit
before orchards were walled and sold?
Who spoke to the hills
before machines drilled their silence away?

In Niyamgiri, they stood before the bulldozers,
said no to the men in suits,
no to the holes blasted into sacred mountains,
no to the factories that feed on the bones of the land.

They stood, as they always have
with nothing but their voices,
with nothing but the right to remain.

The tongue of the land splits into two hundred rivers.
Ho and Mundari in one valley,
Kui and Gondi in another,
Khasi carried by the wind,
Mizo shaped by the rain,
a language for every mountain and every tree,
a way to call the sun into the fields,
a way to mourn the hunt,
a way to speak to the dead.

But in the school, the language does not belong.
It is left at the door, like dust shaken from the feet.
The child speaks in borrowed words,
learns the cost of a mother tongue
measured in silence, in exile, in forgetting.
Yet in the forests, in the hills,
in the clearing where the fires still burn,
the old words wait to be spoken again.

The earth is not a resource
it is a rhythm, a breath, beneath the feet.
Rice, millet, and *madua* grow in time with the rain,
the forest gives what is needed and no more.
The hunt is not a conquest,
it is a prayer to the spirit of the beast,
a pact between hunger and life,
between those who take and those who return.

The gods live in stone and tree,
in the hands that till, in the feet that dance.
The harvest is a song, the rain is an offering.
No scripture is needed for belief,
only the sight of the *mahua* blooming at dusk,
only the sound of the river speaking in the night.
They do not own the land, and so they belong to it.

Gond Songs Shaping the Earth

The trees speak in your tongue,
etched with stories of horned gods
and tigers mid-leap,
where the river bends to listen.

Your hands know the patience of earth,
scratching lines into its skin,
coaxing grain from dust,
mapping the seasons in silence.

The forest hums with the weight of memory,
a language older than stone
whispers of *mahua* blooming at dusk,
the slow breath of sal and teak,
the crackle of leaves under bare feet.

You remember when Bada Dev
supremely breathed fire into the dark,
when the first tree rose from the navel of the void,
sacred *Saja* roots drink from veins of underworld,
its branches touching the skins of gods.

From his breath, the rivers learned to move,
the earth stirred from its slumber,
and the first animals stepped out of his shadow,
each carrying the echo of his voice in their bones.

The seven *pariyas*, spirits of creation,
gathered at the edge of the sky,
their hands shaping the hills,
their feet pressing valleys into the land,
their whispers weaving the names of things
into the wind.

Pardhan singers call him back,
Bana strings trembling under their fingers,
each note lifting lost spirits,
each song the bards' thread,
tying the living to the unseen.

They sing of *Lingo*, the first teacher,
who stole fire from the gods,
taught the people the rhythm of the hunt,
the way to read the forest's quiet warnings,

the way to honor the dead with songs
so they do not wander unseen.
Even now, in the glow of dying embers,
his name lingers,
a chant carried by wind and drum,
a fire that refuses to dim.

Your art, dot and line patterns
Natural pigments, charcoal and fingers,
not ink, not brush, but divine symbols,
but rhythmic energy and ritual,
each dot a footprint of a lost ancestor,
each stroke a tether to the unseen.

The world shifts,
roads carve through sacred groves,
factories rise where millet once stood,
but your stories refuse to vanish.
Even in exile, they weave themselves
into the marrow of the land,
waiting for the next hand
to trace them back home.

The Santhals Who Walked First

They walked before there were roads,
before borders and maps,
before the land had a name.
Their words held the shape of rivers,
a language older than the wind
that curled through the Sal trees.
Even now, Santali lingers on the tongues
of those who refuse to forget.

They learned from the land
from the hush of millet in the wind,
from the patience of iron melting into form.
Hands roughened by the pull of the plow,
feet that read the soil like scripture.
The cities swallowed some,
but the fields still call them home.

Twelve names carve the air
like the flight of a hawk
Murmu, Soren, Marndi, Tudu,
lines drawn in dust and blood,
in rules that hold them together.
The *Manjhi* speaks, the council listens,
and justice walks on bare feet.

Their gods have no temples,
only the hush of the sacred grove,
where *Marang Buru* watches,
where *Jaher Era* cradles the wind.
Fire, stone, the echo of a drum
this is how they pray.
No book can hold what the trees already know.

At *Sohrai*, the cattle are painted,
their horns streaked with red earth,
while the harvest hums in waiting granaries.

At *Baha Parab*, hands press flowers
against the foreheads of gods unseen,
petals curling in whispered offerings.
The *Bongas* move between shadows,
neither feared nor forgotten.

When they dance, the earth remembers.
Tumdak and *Tamak* pulse like a second heart,
Banam sings of ancestors who never left.
Their stories do not rest on pages,
they slip between breaths,
caught in the flicker of firelight,
passed from palm to palm, like seeds.

Their hands do not just till the soil
they trace the world's first murals,
etching birds and beasts onto mud walls,
spinning colors from the earth's marrow.
In the hush before dawn,
a flute weaves through the trees,
a sound that knows no master,
only the longing to belong.

At dawn, they move through rows of green,
hands vanishing into the thick breath of leaves,
fingers plucking, weaving, breaking,
the rhythm of a life bent to another's gain.
In the scent of crushed tea,
in the damp earth beneath their feet,
they remember forests lost to machines,
rivers stilled by unfamiliar names.

Their words now printed in laws
still waver on tongues unfamiliar with power.
The old songs slip between the clatter of cities,
Santali rising, falling, refusing to drown.
Some have climbed beyond the fields,
beyond the villages,
carrying their stories into the halls of men
yet the land still calls them back.

Even in exile, even in struggle,
they remain rooted, unbroken,
like the first trees that saw them walk.

They walked before there were roads,
and even now,
with cities pressing against them,
with history trying to write over their names,
they still walk.
Feet firm. Voices loud.
The first people. The ones who will remain.

Bhils Move Like Rivers

They do not carve their names into stone,
but in the way a bowstring hums, in the way the wind
remembers the shape of a vanished arrow.

The forests knew them first
bare feet pressing stories into the soil,
the whisper of the hunt,
the hush before the strike.
Eklavya, unseen, still draws his bow,
his skill an offering to silence.

They move like rivers,
not bound by maps or kingdoms,
but by the heartbeat of earth itself.

The *Bhili* tongue carries the weight of the past,
words shaped by the hills,
folded into Rajasthani dust,
braided with Marathi rain.
A language that does not ask for permission,
only echoes itself,
again and again,
in the voices of those who refuse to be erased.

In the dance of *Gavari*, spirits slip between shadows,
masks grinning, bodies painted in the language of wind.
Drums speak, feet answer,
night becomes something more than darkness.
A ritual, a reckoning,
the gods arrive, not as idols,
but in the breath of the dancers,
in the tilt of a head,
in the space between heartbeat and myth.

The hands of the Bhils do not rest
they dot the world into meaning,

brushstroke upon brushstroke,
until a story blooms on canvas.
A sky of peacock blues,
a forest made of ochre veins,
a world that pulses beneath the fingertips,
woven from pigments and patience.

The land was once theirs alone,
before the fences, before the roads.
Now, they till it, cut it,
bend their backs under the weight of stolen rivers.
Still, they leave offerings in the wild places
a stone *for Baba Dev*,
a murmur for *Khandoba*,
a whisper to the trees that remember
who they were before the forgetting began.

Once, the hills burned.
Once, the forests bled.
The British came with bullets,
but the Bhils stood
Tantya, slipping through trees

like a whisper of rebellion,
Mangarh, a pyre of defiance.
No monuments hold their names,
but the land knows.
The wind still hums their stories.

Even now, they weave dots into color,
paintings that hold more than pigment,
more than pattern
maps to lost homes,
songs without sound,
a memory of what was,
a prophecy of what will be.

Bhils do not carve their names into stone.
They do not need to.

Buffalo Songs in the Nilgiris

The hills do not remember
when the first feet pressed their slopes,
but the Todas do.
They speak of ancestors
who shaped the grass with their hands,
who led black-horned deities into the morning mist
and called them by names
no outsider could ever learn.

Their voices hum through the Nilgiris,
a tongue older than the wind in the shola forests,
a language carved from stone and silence,
never written, only spoken
passed from palm to palm
like warm buttermilk at dusk.

In the high curves of the Nilgiris,
where the wind does not rush but lingers,
the Todas walk, slow, deliberate
as if listening to the earth hum its old song.

Houses, curved like backs of resting buffaloes,
stitched from cane, bound by patience,
Silence of woodsmoke and whispering wool.
Here, history does not sit in books;
it lives in the fingertips of elders,
ember-glow of stories passed mouth to mouth,
unwritten, unbroken.

Munds rise from the earth, oval and seamless,
woven from bamboo and grass,
no windows to let the night intrude,
only a low doorway,
visitors bending in quiet deference,
as if entering the ribs of an ancient beast,
a space warmed by breath, not fire.

The buffaloes move like shadows across the hills,
heavy with divinity,
their breath warm against the sky's bare chest.
Not cattle, not property
they are ancestors with hooves,
gods draped in black silk,
their milk poured out in slow-spun rituals
that hold the weight of centuries.

A woman steps into marriage,
not to one, but to brothers
bond thick as the milk that foams in wooden churns.
No one questions the weave of it,
just as no one questions
the way the river chooses its own path.

Hands pull needle through cloth,
red and black running, quiet rivers over white,
pukhoor embroidery, stitch by stitch,
a prayer, a memory,
geometries that do not bend to time,
patterns that whisper of buffalo horns,
of sacred hills, of gods whose names
are held only in thread.

When a life ends, the fire is not sorrow
it is release,
the last breath curling like incense
toward the same sky
where buffaloes dream in their sleep.

Even now, as asphalt veins creep closer,
as the forest exhales its last deep sigh,
the Todas walk, slow, deliberate,
listening still.

Earth Remembers Oraon Footsteps

The sal trees bend,
shadows thick with the weight of time.
Oraon hands press into soil,
not to own, not to break,
but to listen
to the breath of roots,
the quiet of rivers that know their names.

The *dhumkach* drum calls out,
a heartbeat echoing through the dusk.
Feet strike the dust in rhythm,
not a dance of performance,
but of return
footsteps speaking to those who walked before.

In the dark womb of the forest,
Mahadev's shrine holds smells of oil lamps,
smoke curling toward the night,
where spirits move unseen but known.
The ancestors are not lost;
they are the rustle of leaves,
the flicker in the fire,
the whisper inside the hunter's breath.

Beyond the trees,
hands carve life into weave and wood
baskets tight as woven stories,
tattoos mapping a body's history,
iron black with the memory of fire.

When the wind carries the hue of harvest,
women turn grain in their palms,
knowing hunger will not enter tonight.
Men walk the forest paths,
their laughter brief, sharp,
a moment stolen before morning's labor.

And when the land is taken,
when the river is walled,
when machines come like insects
with their steel mouths gnawing the hills,
Oraon hands press into soil once more,
not to yield, not to forget,
but to remember. The earth remembers too.

Driftwood and Ancestors

The tide hums an old refrain,
rolling in with the salt-weight of memory.
The Nicobarese walk the shore,
feet pressing into the hush of sand,
where canoes once carried whispers
between islands, between centuries.
Their hands braid palm fronds into shelter,
their voices rise in songs that chase the wind.
The tide rolls in, carrying the language of elders,
etched into the ribs of fallen canoes.
The Nicobarese walk barefoot over shells,
where stories sleep in the hush of the sand.

Deeper inland, the jungle thickens,
its breath damp, tangled, alive.
Here, the Shompens move unseen,
shadows woven between giant roots,
following the slow belly of the island.
They read the veins of leaves,
listen to the river's murmur,
map the world without a compass.
follow the rhythm of hornbills,
their silence older than maps.

What is a border to the man who names the trees?
What is a country to the woman
who smells rain before the sky darkens?
before the monsoon speaks it aloud?

Driftwood gathers along the shore,
bone-white, salt-etched, forgotten.
A child picks up a piece,
traces its worn spine,
as if it were a Nicobarese ancestor's hand
as if it still remembers.
whispers of storms lost in salt.
as if reading a Shompen history
not yet stolen.

Breath of the Heights

The mountain does not bow to footsteps,
but the Sherpa walks where the sky thins,
where the wind unthreads itself against rock.

They do not carry burdens
only the weight of summits,
the breath of ancestors woven into their lungs.

In the thin light of dawn,
they lace their boots with quiet knowing,
tracing paths that have no names,
only the whispers of ice shifting beneath them.

Born to heights, blood thick with altitude,
The Sherpa reads the moods of the Himalayas
when clouds sink too low, when ice cracks a warning.
Fingers tie the prayer flags, red for fire, blue for sky,
green for the forests far below, unseen from ridges.
The prayer flags fray but do not fall,
tangled in the fingers of the wind,
stitching the valley to the gods.

In the stone villages of Nepal,
butter lamps burn, flicker in shadowed shrines,
prayers rising with juniper smoke, dim temples,
In Tibet, they listen to breath of yaks on frozen ground,
a slow rhythm of survival.
The sherpas speak to Sikkimese mountain winds,
in Ladakh, they learn from silence, nor break it.
draw wisdom from stillness, respect its weight.

No conquest, no flag to plant,
only the knowing
the mountain will outlive all footprints,
they are not here to conquer,
but to move with the earth as it rises.

No Songs Left for the Tharus

In the deep swamps of the Terai,
beneath the watchful eye of the sun,
the Tharus, with skin of weathered bark,
tangle their roots in the soil of memory.
Their land breathes with them
Terai rice fields hum their names,
shape of harvests steeped in monsoon's embrace,
and the rhythms of the *dholak*
once stirred the very ground they walked.

But time
unfolds like an old prayer flag,
torn by winds no one asked to blow.
Their songs once rose with the dawn,
now swallowed by the river's murmur
and the chains of unspoken laws.
The Tharu homes
not huts, but cradles of the earth
now overtaken by new roads,
foreign tongues unravel their stories.

Who will remember the harvests?
The sharp scent of wet paddy
the long nights singing with mosquitoes?
Who will recall the wild silence
when the rivers rise
and the forest whispers names
no one speaks anymore?
The birds know them.
But do we?

The women
draped in the sinless hues of dhoti,
once spun from the threads of their own hands
now wear the burden of silence,
the Tharu *rangoli* on the doorsteps fading,
as the wind forgets their names.
Tharu men once carried weight of

bamboo poles, now stand silent, sound of
their labor is lost in the roar of machines.

Who will remember the deep, dark nights
of the *Chhewar* ceremony,

when the young boys, heads shaved,
were sent into the jungle to return as men?
Who will recall the rhythms of the Tharu dance
the beating of the *mahur*,
the clapping hands, the foot stamping
beneath the moon that once watched over
all that was theirs?

The seeds they planted
in the black soil and the floodwaters
are scattered,
lost to those who have forgotten
how to plant with reverence.
And the old trees,
with roots that once knew their names,
now stand barren,
watching with weary eyes.

No longer do they sing the river's song
the one sung during the Holi festival
when they threw colors like promises
against the wide expanse of the sky.
The *mela* no longer calls them together,
the village once lit by oil lamps
now flickers with the cold light of strangers' neon.
Their elders, whose mouths once shaped the stories
of their ancestors' fight with the jungle
and the dance of the *pithauri*
beneath the harvest moon,
are now quiet
their voices cracked like old pottery,
lost to time,
or drowned in the shadows of new borders.

The Tharus are the soil's last cry
silent, unbroken,

but waiting to bloom again,
if only the world would listen.
In the heart of their quiet,
in the space between breath and earth,
the songs they have forgotten
still linger.
And when the rains come,
they will rise again.

Hmong, We Weave

In the highlands of Vietnam, Laos, Thailand, China,
where the mist clings to the ridges,
where rivers carve stories into stone,
the Hmong stitch their histories
into cloth that speaks when voices cannot.

Fingers pull indigo through hemp,
dye deep as the Mekong at dusk,
wax flowing like rivers mapping escape,
each batik line a trail of footsteps
through forests thick with silence.

We weave spirals, paths of return.
We weave squares, fields left behind.
We weave stars, names of ancestors,
unspoken but never lost.

Once, they made us leave the mountains,
but we carry them with us,
stitched into every pleat and fold,
stitched into the hands of daughters
who learn to sew before they learn to write.

Far from the highlands,
in foreign lands with foreign tongues,
the needle still moves,
pulling the past through the eye of the present,
refusing to let us unravel.

Hands that weave are hands that remember.
The loom is not wood, not metal
it is a story stretched taut,
held between a mother's fingers
and the breath of her daughter.

Blue indigo so deep it swallows the sky,
batik lines drawn with wax and fire,
coiling into symbols older than war,
older than exile, older than the names
they whisper only in the mountains.

Silver beads catch the light
coins from a world that tried to forget them.
They sew them into skirts that ripple like rivers,
carrying echoes of footsteps
across borders that never held them.

Each stitch a road back home,
each thread a root too strong to cut.
In the folds of their cloth,
they carry their dead,
their songs, their vanished villages.

The mountains have never been kind,
but they have always been theirs.
And so they weave,
because to weave is to stay,
even when the world says leave.

The fingers move like memory
needle pulling sky into fabric,
stitching histories into cloth
where no words are written.

A mother bends over indigo vats,
dyes deep as river currents,
as if she could hold time there,
as if blue could bind a people
scattered like seeds on foreign soil.

Patterns rise
zigzags of flight, spirals of return,
the story of exile,
the map home sewn into sleeves.

Silver weights dangle at the hem,
not ornaments, anchors.
Listen: they clink like voices,
like the ones left behind.

The looms whisper in the dark,
longing woven tight as war,
as footsteps through bamboo forests,
as the hush of mist in hidden valleys.

A child is wrapped in story cloth,
tiger, river, spirit road,

her fingers trace the stitches,
learning to read the past
before she learns to speak.

Far from the highlands,
in cities of neon and noise,
a grandmother still threads the needle,
sews a mountain into her lap,
refusing to let it disappear.

Sky-Bound Riders

The Mongols do not walk
they ride,
hooves thundering across the steppes,
windswept plains where no wall holds back the sky.

Their yurts breathe with the land,
poles anchored in the bones of ancestors,
felt walls thick with the scent of mare's milk,
the smoke of a thousand winters.

A shaman's drum beats like hooves in the storm,
echoing the voices of wolves,
the firelit hum of old gods
calling to the spirits in the Altai,
whispers rising from Gobi sands,
echoing through the heart of Karakorum.

Their horses do not gallop;
they remember
each hoofprint pressing history
into the throat of the steppe.
The wind does not pass through them;
it kneels. The sky is their ceiling,
the grass their cradle,

Their tents breathe with the earth,
poles anchored in the bones of ancestors,
felt walls heavy with smoke of a thousand winters.

But fences creep where rivers once roamed,
factories rise where wild hooves pounded,
and the children of Genghis
trade the saddle for a city street,
the wind no longer theirs to ride.

They have sung to the sky before nations had names,
before borders were carved like scars on the earth,
and no empire, no wire, no map
no border has ever tamed
a rider of the wind.

The Ones Who Hold the Sky

They were here before the snow learned to fall,
before the Himalayas carved their spines into earth,
before the Yarlung Tsangpo carried prayers to sea.
before the mountains grew their prayer-stitched scars,
before the rivers carried exile in their currents.

Tibet, China, India, Nepal, Bhutan,
names drawn like lines on water,
but the land knows no divisions,
only the rhythm of footsteps crossing borders
that once never were.

Tibetan voices rise with the wind,
not to beg, not to bend,
but to remind the world
that silence is not surrender.

They wrote no borders on the land,
only footsteps, only echoes,
only prayers left to rise
like juniper smoke in the thinning air.

The sky was theirs to hold
a weight carried on backs wrapped in ochre,
feet hardened by the cold logic of stone,
hands pressed together,
not in defeat, but in memory.

From Lhasa's gutted monasteries
to Dharamsala's narrow lanes,
from the mountains of Mustang
to the streets of Thimphu,
they gather remnants of a stolen homeland,
carrying it not in their pockets,
but in the way they bow,
the way they remember.

Now, the earth beneath them shifts,
names erased,
tongues cut from their roots,
monasteries hollowed to whispers
yet still, they walk,
still, they remember,
still, they hold the sky.

Africa: Rhythms of the Earth

Red Thread of the Maasai

Maasai move like flame against the dust,
not lost, never lost
the wind carries their words,
long vowels stretched like sinew,
syllables leaping, hooves over the plain.
names hold the echo of the past,
each phrase an ember of older tongue
refusing to burn out.

Their bodies wear history,
red *shúkàs* folding into the wind,
woven with the breath of ancestors,
stitched with the silence of waiting stars.
Beaded collars, tight against the skin,
circles of sun and storm,
each bead a story,
each story a step toward the fire.

Maasai do not measure wealth in numbers
but in dark-eyed hum of cattle,
in the earth's sounds beneath bare feet,
in hands that build not for one,
but for many.
A house is not a house
unless laughter leaks through the walls,
unless voices gather like rain in a gourd.

Maasai do not flinch when the world shifts,
when roads carve scars into the land,
when cities pull at edges of belonging.
They sing louder,
stamp their feet harder,
etch their bloodlines into the sky,
a red sun rising, never setting
a people who refuse to fade.

Maasai drink tradition from deep wells of time,
never drowning, never letting past slip water-like,
Maasai stand, straight-backed against the wind,
the horizon stretching wide,
never wider than their knowing
never wider than the red thread
that stitches past to present,
present to forever.

Beating Heart of the Zulu

The earth does not forget Zulu steps,
pressed deep by a thousand dances,
warriors who move as if the ground
were an old friend speaking their name.
Drums call, voices rise,
the tongue of kings and storytellers,
clicks and thunder braided together,
a river of sound carving through time.

Zulu bodies carry weight of centuries,
wrapped in the shimmer of beads,
red, blue, white, a covenant,
every thread a strange sense of belonging.
Cowhide shields lean against the wind,
shaped by hands that remember
how to weave war and wisdom
into the same breath.

Zulu man is not only himself
he is his ancestors walking beside him,
he is the women who sing his name into the sky,
he is the children who will shape his shadow
long after he has gone.
The village breathes as one,
a circle unbroken,
where wisdom is passed
like embers from fire to fire,
never letting the night
swallow their light.

Zulu women do not ask the past
They carve it into the present,
into the rhythm of hands molding clay,
into the stomp of feet splitting the dust,
into relics, of empires risen, crumbled.

When the world forgets how to listen,
Zulu remind it with their voices,
with their bodies moving like rivers,
with their names sung through open skies.
not echoes,
not stories locked in brittle pages.
but fire that does not fade nor burn out. Roars.

Ancestral Drums of Yoruba

Air thick with voices older than time,
woven into winds, threads of an ancient loom.
Not words, memories stitched into bones of earth,
footsteps pressed deep into red soil,
ancestors sing through the roots of the Iroko tree.

Here, time does not break apart.
Circles fold the past into veins of the now,
Newborn child carries weight of old names,
Old man walks with the laughter of the yet-unborn.
The world a river, flowing forward, circling back.

Orisha stand at the crossroads, watching.
breath the flesh of the talking drum,
Names sung in fire-lit gatherings,
Stories spill into night, carried by hands of Bata,
Strike against leather calling forth the unseen.

Ogun, the iron-willed, shapes world with his hands,
blade carving destinies, fire making men unbreakable.
Obatala, the sculptor of bodies,
molds spirit into form, white cloth, billowing cloud.
Sango, with thunder in his veins,
splits the sky, rage cleansing, fire reborn in storm.

At the edge of village, women kneel, bowls of water,
invite wisdom of Yemoja, mother of tides,
sweet song moving between worlds,
pull the living toward wisdom of the sea.
Cast cowries onto woven mats,
read the past in scattered bones of future.

Egungun dance in fabric worn from memory,
layers upon layers, hands once held a newborn,
that once closed the eyes of the dying.
To see them is to feel those who walked before,
to know that the dead do not rest,

but move among the living,
stirring the dust, drinking the air,
never gone, only changed.

In the night, voices rise
the chant of the *Babalawo*, tongue
bridge between the visible and the veiled.
Odu Ifa opens like a door,
reveal paths walked by those who once stood here,
by those who will stand here again.

The market rustles, weave of barter and breath,
palm wine tilting, kola nuts cracked between palms.
Cloth, steeped in dusk's marrow, drips indigo
not color, but memory pressed into folds,
wrapped around waists moving like river reeds,
stitched into the rhythm of feet that have never
been still, carried stories across waters,
that have never forgotten
the shape of a journey.

The drum does not speak, it shudders,
a ribcage struck by the hands of history.
The people do not answer, they rise,
spilling their voices into air, shaken calabashes.
And the world, for a moment,
leans in, unsure if it is hearing or being heard,
through the mending of time.

The drum speaks again,
the people answer.
And the world, for a moment,
remembers how to listen.

Voices of the Kalahari

The Kalahari breathes in silence,
a vast, open ribcage of the earth,
where the San footprints weave stories
across Botswana's dunes,
Namibia's red sands,
South Africa's dry riverbeds,
Angola's whispering grass.

San listen
to the crackle of fire,
the sharp click of tongue and tooth,
the wind combing through thorn trees,
naming the land as it moves.

The earth is a drum,
and San walk upon its skin,
bare heels pressing stories
into the dust
a map only wind and San can read.

On cave walls, San hands remember
the shape of the eland,
its body stretched in ochre and time,
its spirit leaping beyond the hunt
into the dreaming world.

The sky folds itself into ember,
spills its light on stone,
where San hands have etched
the memory of beasts
before their hooves were lost
to fences and machines.

San elders speak of a time
when stars were close enough
to touch,
when no border severed the path

of the eland's dreaming hooves.San drink the hush of dawn,
listen to the click of fire,
language of hunger and hunt,
arrows whispering through air,
of rain returning,
sometimes not.

The land tightens, shrinks beneath San,
the rivers forget San names,
the rivers shrink to memory,
fences rise like silent storms,
and the old songs
fade into stone.

The Unwritten Map of the Amazigh

Berbers walk where no road was laid,
where the mountain speaks in stone
and the desert remembers every footprint.

Not a tribe, not a nation,
but a tide, rising and receding,
never lost, never still.

Berbers move like wind-carved dunes,
footsteps pressed into stone and shifting sand,
voices woven in a language older than maps
that failed to name them.

Hands carve stories into cedar and clay,
lines of script curling like windblown sand,
each symbol a threshold
to a home beyond walls.

A song lingers in the weave of carpets,
in the blue stain of indigo robes,
calloused palms that bend copper into light.

In the shade of olive groves,
hands shape clay into vessels,
water slipping over fingers
Berbers have known sword and song.

No boundaries have held Berbers,
no empire has swallowed them whole.
They remain
not ghosts, not echoes,
but the hum beneath the wind,
the unbroken thread of the land.

The desert does not own them
nor mountain nor city, nor borders drawn by
hands never touched the earth with reverence.

Not conquered, not forgotten,
only misread by those who never learned
the alphabet of the wind.

Igbo: The Ones Who Refuse to Vanish

They walked before the land had a name,
before the rivers were told where to run,
before the gods learned how to listen.

They carried their stories in their bones,
in the tilt of their heads,
in the slow, knowing glance of elders
who had seen the world change hands
and refused to let it slip from theirs.

Chukwu, the one beyond naming,
watched from the sky's deep hollow
as hands pressed into the soil,
pulling yams from the belly of Ala,
who never turned her face from them.
A people rooted in what does not break
wood carved into gods,
iron bent into purpose,
body draped in white to meet the ancestors
who never truly leave.

Before shrines slick with oil and knowing,
fire whispered truths wind could hear.
Diviner traced futures in kola nuts,
Bridge between the living and the unseen.
Spirits curled in the roots of ancient trees,
spoke through the slow hiss of rain on bronze altars.
Nothing was empty. Nothing was silent.

The earth hears their footsteps long before they arrive.
In the time of kings without crowns,
when voices wove governance like a net of air,
they sat in circles,
words stacked into walls stronger than any palace.

The wind carries the memory of their leaving,
the forced migrations, the war songs swallowed
before they could be sung. The Igbo do not disappear
They transform. They remain.

They are the ones who name themselves,
who call to their dead and hear them answer,
who kneel in the dust not in surrender
but in conversation

Stone and Sound: The Shona

You carved your name in stone
before the world thought to keep records.
Before time was a tyrant,
before borders were drawn in dust,
you stacked the sky with granite,
one block at a time,
until the walls of Great Zimbabwe
whispered their own defiance.

Hands that shaped kingdoms
now shape serpentine,
chiseling history into smooth curves,
faces emerging from rock,
as if the ancestors
still wish to speak.

The *mbira* sings in the twilight,
its metal tongues remembering
footsteps that once pressed this soil,
prayers lifted with each note
a music that does not beg,
only insists
that memory will not drown.

The *mhondoro* walk unseen,
lion spirits moving through grasslands,
their breath hot in the wind.
They guard the rivers,
call the rain,
and whisper into the dreams of elders,
who wake with the weight of history
pressing their chests.

Firelight flickers on the faces of dead,
not gone, only watching,
only waiting to be honored
in the slow murmur of prayers,

the quiet offering of millet,
the hushed syllables of old names.

Even where the church bells ring,
the old gods listen.
The hymns carry echoes of ancient chants,
and faith is a river with many branches,
some winding through the past,
some rushing forward
to meet the dawn.

The hands that carved kingdoms
also carved fields,
planted sorghum in the dry earth,
coaxed maize to rise from the dust.
Cattle move in the morning light,
lowing like an old song.
Each harvest is a promise kept,
a whispered vow
between earth and those who tend it.

They called your ruins abandoned,
called your voices lost,
but stone does not crumble
for those who still listen.
And the wind, moving through
the broken walls of empire,
remembers your name.

Himba Do Not Vanish

In the Kunene, the land speaks in drought and stone,
the wind carries the smell of cattle and wild earth,
Himba walk, not ghosts, not relics,
but those who belong.

The air is thick with ochre,
Their skin, pressed with *otjize*,
red earth mixed with time,
with butterfat, with the sun's slow fire.
Not paint. Not ornament. But shield, a second skin,
This is the earth, carried like breath,
whisper of ancestors breathing in dust.

Himba do not fade like forgotten dust,
youth braided thick in rhythms of earth,
hair held by the weight of years,
headdresses rising like folded sky.
the married do not ask the wind, a silent witness,
moves, adorned in copper rings,
beads humming around ankles,
goatskin skirts carry the shape of land.
cattle move, ribs press against weight of hunger,
men read the silence of the grass,
listen for water, listen for the voice of the land.
When the land refuses, they do not beg
they follow, they shift, they endure.

In the sacred fire, *Okuruwo*,
the past is not a thing buried.
The flames rise, speaking in tongues of ember and smoke,
calling the spirits, who lean close to listen.
Here, *Mukuru* waits in the glow of burning wood,
here, the dead do not forget the living.

The world arrives with wires and glass-eyed screens,
with hunger to name them disappearing,
to say they are vanishing into history.

But they do not vanish.
Himba press the earth into their skin.

The fire still burns in the dark.
The cattle still move, ribs pushing against the wind.
And the last indigenous keepers of Kunene
stand, unbowed.

The Sabar Beats for the Wolof

They come from the land where the Griot's voice
winds through rivers, tracing the shape of history.
In the dust of old kingdoms, the Jolof empire stood,
the winds remember. They have never forgotten
the deep rumble of the earth when the first drums
struck their call to the stars.

Their blood runs thick with the salt of trade routes
gold, cloth, and the ocean's salt mingling on the skin.
In the silence of moonlit nights, their names
were whispered into the air, the Griots' tongues
wrapped around each syllable, each moment,
binding their stories to memory.
For history cannot lie
it is passed, not in the ink of a page,
but in the pulse of hands on a drum.

Not just by prayer, but in every breath they take
the hues of the *Mouride* brotherhood,
wisdom of *Tijaniyya* unfold like a prayer shawl,
unbroken through generations.
Hearts bound to a path lit by muslim faith,
the divine whispers in rhythms of devotion,
and the soul rises, sways like the Sabar drum.

Dance and song, the Sabar beats
these languages, through bloodlines,
not of words, but of limbs and sound.
A single drum can tell the story of a land,
rhythms tell map of wars fought and victories won.
From the shadows of the drum, Mbalax rises,
Youssou N'Dour's voice entwine with sacred thrum,
a fusion of old and new, the future shaped
by the syncopation of the past.

Each thud an echo of ancient feet
dancing across the same soil that knows their names.
and they and their ancestors, continue
to dance into the future

This is where they come from
a land that has never stopped remembering.

Ochre Hands, Timeless Lands:
Aboriginal Echoes from Australia

Whakapapa: The Blood of the Māori

The wind chants in voice of Tāwhirimātea,
carving legends in the bones of islands.
The rivers run like veins of *tūpuna*,
whispering the names we carry still
Māori, people of the land,
people of the ocean's breath.

We are woven into the flax of time,
mokopuna of warriors, of carvers, of chiefs.
Our *haka* is thunder, fists striking earth,
feet pounding the pulse of Aotearoa.
We shape gods from wood,
etching whakapapa into the grain
each line, each spiral, a name unbroken.

The forests know us, the oceans call us,
the waka still glides in our blood.
We do not stand alone.
Behind us, the bones of our people rise,
the earth rested with their voices,
the sky stretched wide with their gaze.

Ka mua, ka muri
we walk backward into the future,
led by the hands of those who came before.

We are Māori
not a story forgotten,
not a shadow erased,
but a carving deep in the spine of the land,
a chant carried by the wind,
a fire that will never fade.

The wood speaks in language of ancestors,
chisels tracing stories in spirals of memory.
Each *koru* curling toward the sky
a newborn breath, a life unfolding,
a line unbroken.

We do not stand alone. Behind us, the bones
of our people rise. Our whakapapa does not fade.
It is carved into the land, sung into the wind,
etched into our very skin.
the sky stretched wide with their gaze.

Tattooed in the Bones of Samoa

The ocean speaks in waves of memory,
rolling across the backs of our ancestors.
The winds hum the songs of chiefs,
calling us by names inked into time.

We are Samoan, born of fire and tide,
our voices carved into the sky.
The *tatau* etches our stories in blood,
a map of honor across our skin
not just ink, but lineage,
not just marks, but a covenant.

The *malofie* wraps our legs like roots,
anchoring us to the bones of our people.
Each line whispers of service,
To wear it is to bear the weight of Samoa,
to walk with the past stitched into flesh.

The *fale* rises, its pillars breathing,
holding the laughter of old men,
the wisdom of matriarchs,
the echoes of orators whose words
can shake the earth, weave into tides.

We do not stand alone.
Behind us, the voices of *aiga* rise,
the ancestors watching from the misted hills.
To be Samoan is to be many,
to be bound by blood, by duty, by love.

The ocean calls, and we answer.
The *tatau* bleeds, tells our stories.
The ancestors watch, and we remember.
For we are Samoa,
tattooed in the bones of the land,
etched forever in the song of the sea.

Yet here we stand, in cities of glass,
our voices strong in foreign lands.
We carry Samoa in boardrooms, in stadiums,
in classrooms where wisdom takes root.
We walk two worlds, one in the past,
one in the now, never divided, never lost.

The Palawa Are Still Here

The wind moves through the button grass plains,
carrying the breath of those who walked before.
Footprints linger where none can see,
pressed deep into the ochre-streaked earth.

The kanamaluka river knows our names.
It speaks them in the hush of morning mist,
in the pull of the tide at *larapuna*,
in the quiet language of stone and water.

They said we were gone,
that our voices had fallen silent,
our people erased by time, hands that did not belong.
But the land does not forget.
It holds our stories in the ochre-painted rock shelters,
in the middens where shells still whisper of old feasts,
in the fire-hardened spears that once struck

wallabies on the hunt.

We gather by the fire,
hands shaping words once stolen from our tongues.
Palawa kani rises from silence,
stitched together from memory,
a language reborn, carried in song,
each syllable a defiance,
each word a homecoming.

On the shores of *takayna,*
we trace the same paths as our ancestors,
where bark canoes once sliced through the water,
where women dove for *abalone*, gathered muttonbirds,
where stars still guide us as they always have.

We are not relics.
We are not echoes.
We are Palawa
keepers of the fire, children of salt and wind,
walking forward, unbroken,
with the past at our backs
and the future in our hands.

The Noongar Dreaming: Boodja's Breath

The land speaks without sound or word,
in the deep cracks of ancient rock,
memory carried in wind sweeping across boodja
the land that remembers us,
that holds us in its breath.

Here, the Boodja is not just earth,
it is a vast body, its rivers veins,
its forests lungs, its mountains eyes
that see beyond the horizon.
To walk here is to walk in Dreaming,
to follow the paths drawn by the hands of those before,
to move with the rhythms of an earth that remembers.
The hills know our names,
and the wind carries our songs
not forward, but back,
to when time had no edge, only connection.

We do not look to the stars for our past
we walk on it.
Stories of our ancestors not whispered from sky,
but rise from beneath our feet,
in the rhythm of the *djidi-djidi* bird's call,
in the silence of the *wandoo* tree standing tall,
in the bones of those who've walked this land long before us.

Dreaming is not a vision of the past,
it is the heartbeat of this land, woven
into the dirt, the water, the sky.

The names of rivers,
the shapes of hills,
the space between the trees
they are stories,
alive in the blood that runs through us,
in the pathways we trace without thinking.

The *Noongar Dreaming* does not fade,
it does not wait for us to understand.
It is the song we hum quietly under our breath.
It is here, in us,
and in the land that has always known us.

Fiji's Silent Song

Under the shade of ancient banyans,
a circle forms on Fiji's soft earth,
feet kiss soft earth that has held the weight
of warriors' feet and ancestors' songs.

The *meke* begins, no words spoken
a dance carries centuries of stories,
hands weaving forgotten battles,
of spears raised beneath the moon's gaze,
and the smell of *yaqona* thick in the air.

A cup, dark and earthy, passed
roots spread deep within Fiji's heart,
where ancestors' voices course through veins
of every island, weight of waves that crash.

The warriors' blood lingers in the rhythm,
in the beat of drums, heartbeat of the earth,
in the sway of hips, bodies that tell their tales,
in the stillness of the ocean's breath,
where blood and salt collide, merge,
where spirit of Fiji rises with sun's first light.

In the stillness, the land sings without sound,
breath braided into the river's slow turn,
in each grain of sand, each leaf, each stone,
where the past leans into the future
like the moon holds the tide, gripping earth
a song untethered, neither lost nor claimed
belongs to no one, felt in the bones,
but to all who listen with their souls.

The *lali* drum speaks in thunder and tremor,
its voice a river pulling time backward,
chants rise, thick as the scent of crushed *yaqona*,
bare soles weave, stars smolder in the hush,
hands slicing air like wind-split waves,
the sweat of dancing bodies, flame fed
by island's breath, warriors into the earth.

Tonga: The Weight of Names

The eldest speaks,
and the air folds around his words,
heavy with the breath of ancestors.
His name is not his alone
it is a tether, a burden, a cresting wave.

A younger man lowers his eyes,
his own name still light, still waiting
for the weight of history to anchor it.
Here, rank is the rhythm of the tide,
pulling forward, pulling back,
never uncertain, never still.

The priest touches the ground
before he rises,
his hands remembering the first fire,
the first kava bowl offered to gods
who still listen from the roots of trees.
His voice does not belong to him
but to the lineage carried in his bones.

A poet stands at the edge of a gathering,
words rising from his chest like salt wind,
braiding praise and grief
in a language deeper than the ocean.
His syllables hold the kingdom upright,
his verses feed the silence between kings.

In Australia, they walk in two worlds
their sandals leaving prints in the red earth,
the sea is never far.
Their names shift here, forgotten tongues.
slipped between syllables of a new land,
They hold their past like a mirror,
the sunlight bending, reflecting
in the sunburnt horizon.

Everything here is a vessel
a name, a prayer, a poem
and each must be carried
with steady hands.

Resistance and Survival:

The Struggle for Rights

The Ones Who Walk Before the Road

They do not ask the forest for permission
they were here before the trees learned
to stretch toward the distant blue sky,
before rivers carved their names into the earth.

Their tongues hold the first salt of speech,
words shaped by wind and fire,
by millet crushed under stone,
by drumbeats that pulse like a second heart.

In the shadow of machines, they do not disappear.
They stand, feet buried in soil
that was never sold, only taken.
The land remembers them,
though men in white offices do not.

They walk without footprints on roads
that are not theirs,
past fields that once fed them,
past hills where spirits have grown silent.
In the city, their names are misspelled,
their voices thinned to whispers.
They are asked to become something else,
to unlearn the memory of fireflies,
to unmake the stories stitched into their hands.

They do not.

They carry their gods in the creases of their palms,
in the way they call to the earth before they cut a tree,
in the songs that do not need paper to exist.

And even if the road stretches on forever,
even if the maps erase them,
they will still be here
standing in the places where no monuments rise,
where the wind still speaks their names.

The land remembers their footprints, but not the laws

forests cleared, rivers rerouted, hills hollowed for ore.
Evictions inked in contracts they never signed,
schools too distant, medicines priced out of reach.
They hold their names like embers, refusing to fade.

Borrowed From Tomorrow

The earth remembers its first footsteps
soft impressions of moccasins,
bare soles kissing soil with reverence,
a dialogue unbroken between skin and stone.

The rivers carry stories in their curves,
not veins of commerce,
but whispers of ancestors whose prayers
grew wings in the mist of every dawn.

Forests do not stretch their arms to timber;
they cradle the unseen,
their shadows a sanctuary,
their roots tangled with secrets
older than any map can claim.

Mountains rise not as borders
but as keepers of sky-reaching truths
their spines bending only for
the songs carved by first hands
on the cliffs of memory.

Who owns the wind
that braids through a child's hair?
Who owns the rain
that baptizes her face?

First rights are not written
on parchment or stone;
they are etched in the pulse of the land,
in the fire that refuses to forget.

This earth, borrowed from tomorrow,
was never a prize to conquer
but a promise to uphold—
to the ones who first called it home,
whose spirits remain
woven into its breath.

Voices Beneath the Soil

They do not walk; they weave.
Threads of bare feet stitch the earth's damp skin,
Binding root to root, stone to stone,
Until the forest hums, memory of their passing.

Their voices are the slow drip of resin,
Their silences, the call of cicadas
Breaking open the shell of dusk.
The wind bends to them,
Carry whispers of mahua blossoms
And the salt of unspoken histories.

The river does not flow past them;
It pauses, pooling in their reflections,
Its surface fractured into shards of sky.
They drink its laughter,
Spit it back as song.

Civilizations hover, birds afraid to land,
Their shadows casting doubt on
The sun-streaked shoulders of those
Who build nothing they cannot leave behind.

Ash settles where fire once danced,
The forest remembers the shape of flame,
The scent of charred stories rising.
It cradles their echoes in hollowed trees,
Where owls blink and know.

To see them is not to understand them.
They are not what is left behind,
But what the earth hides,
What it clutches to its chest
When the sky grows heavy with forgetting.

The Forest Breathes Them

They walk where the earth remembers,
Each step a whisper to the roots, each gesture
A dance with the wind's unbroken tongue.
Adivasis, keepers of stories older than silence,
Speak not in words but in the ache of rivers,
The rhythm of mountains, the quiet fury
Of trees bearing scars from centuries unseen.

Their skin holds the map of forgotten rain,
Cracks where the sun has kissed too hard,
Lines drawn by hands that never asked permission.
Their laughter rises like smoke,
A signal to the sky
That nothing can steal their fire.

Civilizations build over their songs,
Brick by brick,
Like a blind man stacking stones over a river.
Yet the forest breathes them back into itself,
Its leaves murmuring their names long after
Axes silence their voices.

They are the thrum beneath asphalt,
The memory under cement.
Not broken, but reshaped;
Not erased, but waiting
In the curl of a river,
In the rebellion of an uncut tree,
In the defiant arch of a bird's flight.

To call them primitive, to
Name the roots unworthy of the tree.
To turn from the soil's quiet wisdom,
The unseen heartbeat of ancestry.
They are not what history writes,
But what history forgets to bury.
The breath between forgotten pages,
The soul of a story still unwritten.

Resistance and Survival

We are the fire beneath your feet,
not the flicker that would disappear,
the ember burning when the wind is still.
We are the stone that sits unyielding
when your machines try to grind it to dust.

You thought we would be swallowed
by your towers of glass,
our voices lost in the hum of greed.
we are the voice beneath the pavement,

We carry the sun in our eyes,
the mountain in our hands,
the river in the hollow of our chest.
Our stories etched in earth's bones,
written in the language of roots
that snake through the soil
long after concrete cracks, crumbles.

We do not ask for your forgiveness
for the land you have defiled,
nor your laws that never knew us.
We are the breath that rises
when you bury the air in smoke,
the thunder that answers
when you silence the sky.

You cannot erase the rain
on a desert that was barren,
the music in the howl of wolves
you called wild and unnecessary.
We are the song of the unseen,
the shadows that linger
with walls built too high.

We are not the past
you try to bury beneath progress,
not the memory of a people

you thought would fade.
We rise like the tide,
unbroken, unbowed,

because the earth remembers.

Infinite Hearth

Hearth is not a beginning,
not a roof raised upon beams,
nor doorway swinging open to let you in.
older than timber,
older than clay
threading through air,
silent music between breath and stone,
precedes the first story told
endures beyond the last.

Across India, Gond and Santhal
smell wet earth after the monsoon,
sal forests open like green cathedrals.
Home, drumbeat of festivals,
mahua flowers ferment honeyed drink,
painted walls, animals leap alive in pigment.
The Bhil's courtyard, a cosmos of color -
dot and line of continuity.

Nagas listen for the long horn at dawn,
smell bamboo smoke curl from hearths,
taste rice beer,
voices braided with hills, echo
like a second heartbeat.

Khasi hear rainfall, hollows of mountains,
mossy steps slick with mist,
betel leaves fragrant beneath open sky,
living root bridges swing, quiet strength.
Mizo trace bamboo flutes along streams,
laughter curving with clouds,
fires crackle, stories of shifting hills,
huts hum with remembrance.

Todas feel velvet grass underfoot,
herd-bulls graze beneath Nilgiri mist,
milk churned by hand, whisper to the hills,

ceremonial embroidery folding sky into cloth.
Home stretches across forest, plateau, river, hill,
landscape stitched, breath and ritual,
ancestors moving between body and earth.

Across oceans, Diné home hums in four

sacred mountains, rust-red glow at dawn,
flute carried by desert wind,
bitterness of juniper smoke rising to the sky.
Sandstone holds warmth of the day,
cooling, as coyotes sing evening home.

Acoma breathe belonging, mesa's skin,
tongues taste the salt of roasted corn,
hands roughened by clay vessels
remember the touch of generations
inhale is tethered to the horizon,
exhale returns the sky to itself.

Quechua whisper to Pachamama,
cold air in Andes stings lungs,
coca leaves on tongue steady
for dialogue with mountains.
Alpaca wool brushes skin, a second warmth.
Chaski runner's footfalls drum
message through thin air,
each step a prayer.

Mapuche carry fire, their veins
smoke of burning wood,
metallic tang of river fish on open flame,
songs rising rough as the wind,
defiant, ancestral, echoing
in valleys that refuse silence.

Far south and east, Aboriginal songlines
sung with breath, shake the didgeridoo.
Red dust coats soles of feet,
sun tasting of iron in the mouth.
Waterholes gleam with sweetness beyond thirst.

Each dune, stone, glimmering horizon
syllable in a hymn only earth remembers.

Inuit know home shifts with ice.
Tongue tastes seal oil's depth,
hands grip smooth curve, bone-carved tool.
Drums through igloos, snow-bright silence.
Aurora ripples, great spirit's cloak,
paint skies with green fire.

Not a dwelling,
chorus of landscapes,
convergence of skies.
where the sacred listens,
footprints fuse with memory,
language grows from the ground.

To belong is to kneel with Bhil brushstroke,
to climb with the Quechua breath,
to walk with Aboriginal song,
to stand still with the Diné wind,
to glide with Inuit silence.

Not place but presence,
not structure but resonance,
the fire in the bone,
drumbeat of the earth's skin,
taste of survival,
smell of persistence,
sound of voices unbroken.
unbroken across tribes and time,
a single, infinite hearth.

Dr Nishi Chawla is an academic, a writer and a filmmaker. Nishi Chawla has published ten plays, three novels, and eight collections of poetry. She has also written and directed four award winning art house feature films. She has also co-edited two global anthologies of poetry published by Penguin Random House: 'Greening the Earth' and 'Singing in the Dark.' Dr Nishi Chawla holds a doctorate in English from the George Washington University, Washington D.C., and her post-doctorate from the Johns Hopkins University, Baltimore, Maryland. After teaching for nearly twenty years as a tenured Professor of English at Delhi University, India, Nishi Chawla had migrated with her family to a suburb of Washington D.C. She has taught English Literature for forty years at the University level. She is one of the few Indian playwrights to have two plays in Manhattan, NY. She is the third Indian poet ever to be invited for a reading and a discussion of the US Library of Congress organized, 'The Poet and the Poem' program.

www.ingramcontent.com/pod-product-compliance
Lightning Source LLC
Chambersburg PA
CBHW051835090426
42736CB00011B/1812